Land
and
Liberty

Land
and
Liberty

The Mexican Revolution (1910–1919)

IRVING WERSTEIN

COWLES BOOK COMPANY, INC. NEW YORK

*This book is for
Dr. Eleanore Hayden and Ronnie Keegan,
who remained our steadfast friends
in a time of deep trouble.*

Contents

PART

I

The Dictator

EL PRESIDENTE'S FIESTA

An American visitor to Mexico City in September 1910 wrote to a friend back home: "I'm having a hot time in the old town! They're throwing a shindig that is supposed to last for a whole month. What do you think of that? Music, lights, wine, and beautiful senoritas galore! You'd better make tracks south of the border before this fiesta is over. I'm supposed to be here on business, but am having more fun than I can remember. Come on down for the time of your life!"

This one businessman's ardent opinion was echoed by the many thousands who had flocked to Mexico City that merry and memorable month of September.

The celebrating had a double purpose. The first was to commemorate the one hundredth anniversary of Mexico's declaration of independence; the second, to celebrate President Porfirio Diaz's eightieth birthday and thirtieth year in office.

Although Diaz bore the title *El Presidente* (the President), a more appropriate one would have been *El Dictador* (the Dictator). He had not held on to his office for so long by dispensing democracy. Indeed, he ruled over Mexico like a medieval despot. Those rash or foolish enough to have opposed him in the past frequently had wound up in front of a firing squad.

"I know what Mexico wants and needs," El Presidente once announced. "Anyone who disagrees with that is a traitor and will be dealt with accordingly. . . ."

For three decades, this had been Diaz's credo. During those years he was the dominant figure of his native land. He seemed to be an immutable part of the Mexican scene, along with the valleys and mountains, the deserts and jungles, the wealth and poverty. Diaz was Mexico; Mexico was Diaz.

In September 1910, he was determined to celebrate extravagantly his birthday and the nation's. "I have dedicated my life to my country," he said. "My fate and Mexico's are eternally entwined. I have served my beloved country for most of my days on earth; I hope to continue serving her until my last breath!"

This inspired a Mexico City humorist to quip, "Diaz has been president so long that his portrait should be woven into our flag along with the eagle and the serpent."

But as preparations got under way for the elaborate September festival, some observers noted faint murmurs of discontent in the land, like the distant rumblings of a long dormant volcano about to erupt.

If Diaz was aware of the ominous warnings, he gave no sign. Perhaps, years before, when he was keen and alert, he would have reacted to stamp out the embers of dissent before they ignited. But he had grown old and soft; so had his closest henchmen.

Not a man in the president's cabinet was under sixty. Governors, generals, judges, and police chiefs—almost every minion of officialdom—were in their declining years. No young men with fresh ideas had a place in the Diaz administration. Long ago, El Presidente had surrounded himself with devoted followers whom he had rewarded well for serving him faithfully. They had been the power in the land for decades, but they were growing enfeebled.

Because Diaz excluded youth from his regime and stayed with his old followers, a wide gap separated him

4

from the generation that had grown up since first he became president. The youth of Mexico received none of the benefits Diaz showered upon his associates. Only the lowest government posts were open to an ambitious young man. Those with outstanding skills and talents, men who could have been invaluable to Diaz, had no chance of breaking into the president's inner circle. Eventually it was those frustrated youths who mounted opposition to Diaz.

In September 1910, the dissidents were staying under cover. They protested in whispers, not shouts. But the time was approaching when they would dare come out in the open for a showdown with El Presidente and everything he stood for.

However, that September, only the keenest observers could detect discord in Mexico. On the surface, at least, it seemed that every citizen of the Republic revered Diaz and wanted to take part in the festival.

El Presidente spared neither labor nor money to make the celebration a time to be long remembered. Millions of pesos were lavished on the festivities—far more than the annual budget for education. All sorts of spectacular events were on tap to mark the occasion.

Every night a costly fireworks display lit the skies over Mexico City. The capital was transformed into a fairyland of lights and color. Along the wide avenues every building was bedecked with green, white, and red bunting—the national colors. Flags fluttered from rooftops, windows, and balconies. Magnificent flowered arches curved across the broad Paseo de la Reforma, Mexico City's main boulevard. Hanging in cages from the floral arches were many varieties of brilliantly plumaged tropical birds whose shrill shrieks could be heard above the street din.

A massive cleanup campaign had been launched in the capital. Thousands of laborers swept the streets, whitewashed curbstones, hosed down sidewalks, and re-

5

moved trash. Additional street lighting was installed and at midnight major thoroughfares appeared to be lighted by the midday sun.

As the capital was getting its face lifted, the government invited distinguished persons from Europe, South America, the United States, and Asia to attend the September festivities. Since Diaz was footing the bill for expenses, the foreign turnout was large.

So generous was El Presidente that he even furnished proper formal wear to shabbily attired representatives of poverty-stricken Central American countries. But there were limits to the handouts the regime would tolerate. Mexico City, long noted as a mecca for beggars and panhandlers, was cleared of the ragged mendicants who usually haunted the fashionable districts.

Diaz wanted his foreign guests to be impressed by what they saw in Mexico. "Poverty and rags do nothing to enhance our country's image. During the month of September, beggars, vagrants, and other undesirables will not be permitted entry into the central districts of the city," El Presidente proclaimed.

His police and soldiers obeyed the order to the letter. Patrols rounded up beggar hordes and carted them away from the capital. Also excluded were *peóns*, the peasants who worked the land of wealthy landlords.

For the month of September, at any rate, evidence of poverty, hunger, and human wretchedness did not exist in Porfirio Diaz's Mexico. Foreigners would see none of the hunger and squalor rampant in Mexico.

Magnificent banquets were held almost nightly. Especially imported French chefs prepared the food. "Every meal was a feast," an Englishman reported. The guests ate from solid gold plates with utensils fashioned of the purest silver by Mexico's most talented artisans. Each night, singers, actors, dancers, magicians, acrobats, and other entertainers performed on stages set up in the city's squares and plazas.

"Mexico City was a carnival around the clock," a visitor remembered. "Everywhere one turned, he heard music—guitars, flutes, maracas, violins. . . . The weather held perfect. Warm in the daytime, pleasantly cool after sunset. What a glorious way to spend the hours, eating, drinking, dancing . . . that September, Mexico City was a place of untrammeled pleasures."

Even more gratifying to Diaz than the swarm of distinguished foreigners were the numerous gifts he received from various countries. Nations bestowed upon him bejeweled medals, ceremonial swords, gem-encrusted daggers, awards, citations, and honors.

The biggest delegation came from the United States. Businessmen, senators, congressmen, governors, and mayors swarmed south of the border. According to one man, he had come solely to thank Diaz for having made it easy to do business "down Mexico way." By their own admission, most of the Americans were there to "raise hell and paint the town red."

The wave of warm feelings that radiated to foreigners turned a bit cooler where Americans were involved. Uncle Sam's nephews could not quite break their bigot's mentality about Mexicans. To them, all Mexicans were "greasers." An American was overheard saying, "Diaz is a damned fine greaser. He knows his oats!" Talk of this kind naturally displeased any Mexican within earshot.

Accordingly, Mexicans resorted to their own private insult by labeling every American a *gringo*—an uncomplimentary term that had come into usage during the 1845–48 war with the United States.

However, few untoward incidents marred the proceedings. Guests from points as far off as Japan continued to arrive. Great Britain, still in mourning for King Edward VII, did not send a delegation, although the prime minister cabled a congratulatory message to Diaz.

A high point in the program was reached on Sep-

tember 15, Diaz's birthday. The following day marked
the hundredth anniversary of the beginning of the country's fight for independence. El Presidente's birthday
featured a parade with floats depicting Mexican history
from the time of the Aztec ruler Montezuma to independence. Ten thousand marchers, including fifty full-blooded
Aztecs, strode past the reviewing stand in the big plaza
called the Zocalo. Ironically, some four centuries earlier,
a great Aztec temple had occupied that very spot.

The day closed with a banquet held at the National
Palace. It was attended by sixty world notables, who
dined sumptuously on a ten-course dinner while Diaz
beamed expansively from his place at the head of the
table. As the banqueters were eating off gold and silver
plates, a throng congregated outside the National Palace, packing the Zocalo.

Sixteen bands entertained the crowd, each tootling
a different tune at the same time. To this musical ca-
cophony was added the crackling, banging, and whoosh-
ing of an incredible fireworks display. Rockets left red
trails in the evening sky. Pinwheels whirled. Multicolored
lights flashed. Roman candles popped. The climax of the
pyrotechnical show was a device that exploded with an
ear-shattering bang, shot out multicolored fireballs, and
then formed a twinkling Mexican flag in green, red, and
white sparklers.

At about the moment the flaming banner was glowing in the darkness, a trumpet sounded in the palace
banquet hall. A hush fell over the assemblage. Drum-
mers beat a long roll and spotlights centered on a velvet-
draped balcony. The curtains parted to reveal Mexico's
Liberty Bell, which had signaled the start of the War of
Independence on September 16, 1810. Father Hidalgo,
the parish priest of Dolores, a little town in Guanajuato,
had rung it to call patriots to fight for freedom from
Spain.

In 1896, the church bell of Dolores had been brought

to the National Palace, where it had remained. Once a year *it* was rung to celebrate Mexico's freedom. On that centenary anniversary, those who heard it peal, as Diaz struck it three times with a silver hammer, claimed that the bell sounded louder than ever before.

The festival of September 1910 wound up at the National Palace with a ball that overshadowed all that had gone before. The commodious open-air patio of the palace was roofed over and hung with thousands of roses whose sweet scent perfumed the air. Hundreds of Japanese lanterns illuminated the scene for two thousand beautifully garbed guests who danced to the tunes of a 150-piece orchestra, drank innumerable magnums of champagne, and devoured an unknown amount of canapés.

El Presidente, white-haired and dignified in an impeccably tailored full-dress suit, smiled and nodded to the dancers from his chair in the presidential box. Neither he nor anyone else could know that this was the last time he would preside over an affair in the National Palace.

- 2 -

A NATION ENCHAINED

Diaz had ignored the rumors and whispers of discontent in the land. Instead, he chose to believe that nothing was wrong. Like all dictators, Diaz had created his own truths and his own realities. So badly had he misjudged the situation that within eight months of the magnificent ball his regime was overthrown and he was living out the final years of his life in exile.

Throughout Mexico's history, wide social and economic differences had stratified Mexican society. There was no understanding, no empathy, and no communication between the upper and lower classes.

Small wonder that certain young Mexican intellectuals, sent off to school in Europe and the United States, were shocked when they tasted something of democracy. These youths were quick to see the inequalities that existed in their homeland. Though they had been born to the best Mexico could offer, these maverick idealists often started talking about bringing democratic reforms into their country. It was these upper-class youths who fanned a budding rebellion against Diaz, a rebellion that would be carried on by the oppressed masses.

With a touch of historical irony, the rebel aristocrats calling for a new freedom in Mexico raised the slogan "Universal Suffrage and No Reelection!" They wanted a vote for every eligible Mexican and a law to prohibit a president from serving more than two terms. The irony was that Diaz had come to power many years before on the strength of the same slogan.

In his youth, El Presidente had known hardship and bitter struggle. His life had been difficult almost from the start. He was born in 1830 of mixed Indian and Spanish parentage during a cholera epidemic that raged in Oaxaca, his native town. Many infants died that year, but Porfirio, showing the toughness he would display in later life, passed that terrible time unscathed.

He grew to manhood seemingly unable to find his place in life. A good student, he initially studied for the priesthood but then switched to law. Only partially successful as a lawyer, Diaz found his real vocation when he joined with Benito Juarez, a fellow Oaxacan, in a revolt against the French occupation of Mexico by Maximilian, the Austrian emperor that Napoleon III of France had imposed upon the Mexicans.

Diaz proved to be an outstanding soldier and a dedicated patriot. He was wounded twice and captured three times by the enemy, but escaped each time. After the French were driven out, Diaz emerged from the conflict as a top hero of the newly founded Mexican republic.

Not only was he noted for bravery, but also for honesty, a rare quality in Mexican politicians of that day. During the fighting Diaz had been entrusted by Juarez with a large sum of money to purchase military supplies. When the hostilities ended, he had more than 87,000 pesos left and promptly returned the money to the national treasury, an act unheard of in the rampant graft and corruption of the period.

Porfirio Diaz was a great favorite of Juarez, the president of Mexico. Diaz admired him, but when Juarez, who believed that only he could guide Mexico, sought reelection for a fourth term in 1871, Porfirio opposed him and tossed his own hat in the ring. A third candidate, Sebastian Lerdo de Tejada, also ran that year.

Because no candidate received a majority at the polls, the choice was left up to Congress, which picked Juarez. Lerdo was mollified by an appointment as chief justice of the Supreme Court. The sorely frustrated Diaz refused all favors from Juarez. Gathering some followers, he tried to foment another revolution. But the Diaz uprising of 1871 was swiftly put down by Juarez. Disguised as a priest, Porfirio fled to the north of Mexico and went into hiding.

By the early spring of 1872, Juarez seemed to be steering Mexico into a long stretch of peace and prosperity. For the first time since the war with the French, the land knew calm and tranquillity. But that July, Juarez dropped dead of a sudden heart attack. His passing caused a wild scramble to succeed him in office. Lerdo, the head of the Supreme Court, stepped into the presidency of the Republic.

Four years later, in 1876, Lerdo actively sought reelection. Meanwhile, Diaz, who had gathered a following in the north, rebelled again, raising the slogan "Universal Suffrage and No Reelection!" At the outset, he met reverses, but was such a splendid organizer and campaigner that he finally prevailed. On November 21, 1876, Diaz rode into Mexico City and entered the National Palace where he would hold sway for so long.

Once ensconced, Diaz demonstrated to all that he was in charge. He ruled like a despot, binding together various elements of the Mexican populace in blatant dictatorial fashion. "Those who are not for me are against me!" he announced. "My friends will flourish, my enemies will die!"

Mexicans had known little liberty or democracy since expelling the Spanish in 1821. Because they had experienced vicious repression under a succession of cruel, corrupt, and cynical leaders, the people accepted Diaz, the strong man, the proponent of law and order.

An amendment to the constitution kept Diaz from seeking reelection in 1880. He was succeeded by Manuel Gonzalez, his former minister of war. Under Diaz, graft and corruption had been limited to a highly privileged few. But with Gonzalez, the national treasury became a piggy bank for grafters. Gonzalez was more corrupt than the worst money grabbers in the land.

"Few governments have furnished a more conspicuous example of administrative corruption," a historian wrote of the Gonzalez regime. "The looting of the exchequer was . . . complete and shameless. All revenues went to fill the coffers of Gonzalez and his favorites. . . . The wages of civil servants were suspended. The army alone received its pay . . . otherwise revolution would have broken out."

The Mexican people turned to Diaz again in 1884 and overwhelmingly voted him into the presidency. His predecessor, Gonzalez, left office a rich man. The treasury was all but cleaned out, and even on his last day in office Gonzalez could not resist one more bit of larceny.

He took with him most of the furniture in the National Palace.

President Diaz, on reassuming his post, went through the motions of punishing Gonzalez, but that swindler was an old friend and got off with little more than a mild public reprimand.

For the first years of his regime, Diaz was popular. Although the reforms he had promised did not materialize, people somehow believed that El Presidente would keep his word and bring on an era of economic and social betterment for the masses.

Land for the landless, Diaz had promised; bread for the hungry; personal liberty for all; a fair deal for the oppressed Indians. But at the same time he promised the landowners that their vast estates would not be broken up; that taxes for the rich would remain low; that businessmen would receive preferential treatment; that foreign investors would be encouraged and protected. To laborers and industrial workers, he promised better pay, working conditions, and the recognition of trade unions. But to employers he promised to keep wages down and hours long and to allow no trade unions.

If nothing else, Porfirio Diaz was an adroit politician whose credo was, "Promise something to everybody and give nothing to anyone." He knew how to create the illusion that he was satisfying all, and he was a master at making people believe that he was supporting every cause. Diaz played one group against the other, one faction against the other. Divide and rule was his theme, and it always worked. But after a while even his most ardent backers had to admit El Presidente was no liberal; the individual freedoms he had promised had only been bait to get him elected.

Still, Diaz did give Mexicans something for which they had long yearned. After his return to office in 1884, the country entered a prolonged period of internal peace. During most of his time in office, Mexico enjoyed do-

13

mestic tranquillity, no mean achievement in a land where for generations problems had been settled with guns. The wily Diaz offered the country *pan* or *palo*— bread or a club. To some he held out the lure of wealth and prestige. Some men he bought with gifts of large estates called *haciendas*. Some he won over by granting them political concessions and special privileges. To others, he doled out government jobs or else paid for loyalty in hard cash. Landlords, clergymen, army officers, intellectuals, and even chiefs of outlaw bands took up his offers. The numbers of the Porfiristas grew daily. Those who bowed to Diaz profited. They lived well, enjoying the full benefits of his regime. Those who chose *palo*—the club— lost everything, and either fled or died.

A man of lesser ambition than Diaz would have used his dictatorial powers to enrich himself. But Porfirio did not lust for money; he wanted only power. He spent millions to retain the dictatorship that meant more to him than anything else in the world. He squandered the nation's funds to ensure his hold on the country. Any man, great or small, whom he believed could help him was recruited to attain this goal.

Under Diaz, bandit gangs, which had been committing depredations throughout Mexico for years, were hunted down. When the outlaws were in custody, they were given the choice of *pan* or *palo*. Either they served Diaz or were killed.

Those who opted for *pan* received amnesty and were enrolled into El Presidente's elite police force, the *Guardias Rurales,* a Mexican version of the Canadian Mounties. The former criminals, now splendidly armed, fed, mounted, and uniformed, were singularly effective in tracking down other bandits who had lacked the sense to join Diaz.

The Rurales had license to loot, rob, rape, and shoot with immunity assured. Anything was permissible, just as long as they eliminated outlawry and kept the countryside free of crime. Of course, any worker or peon who objected to his conditions of labor or his wages, any intellectual who voiced a dissenting opinion about Diaz, would promptly be labeled a bandit and have a price put on his head.

Diaz instituted what was called the *ley fuga*, the law of flight. This permitted the police, army, or Rurales to shoot a prisoner and to give the excuse that he had been "shot while trying to escape." More than ten thousand men and women were killed in that fashion during Diaz's regime. The *ley fuga* was little better than legalized murder, but the crime was covered by the excuse that the victim was "running away from justice." This was a most convenient way to eliminate enemies and potential enemies of the regime.

In 1887, El Presidente clamped down even more stringently. He steamrollered through Congress an amendment to the constitution that authorized a second term for the president. Three years later, the ordinance was rewritten to allow an indefinite number of reelections.

Diaz also severely restricted the freedom of the press. He announced that criticism of the chief of state was forbidden. Any journalist or editor disregarding this ruling was denounced as a traitor, and to enforce it Diaz put on his payroll a gang of hardened criminals known as *bravi*. These cutthroats acted as censors for the dictator. Any newspaper editor, writer, or journalist bold enough or foolish enough to defy the regime was visited by an action squad of *bravistas* and either wound up in prison, or was beaten or assassinated.

Courts were notoriously crooked in Diaz's Mexico. Almost every judge in the land was for hire, and justice was a farce. An American resident of Mexico wrote his family in Chicago:

Justice here is really far more satisfactory than in the U.S. . . . Back home you're never sure how your case will come out. Here, you can be damned sure of the verdict if you cross Diaz. In any other sort of case, you know precisely how much to pay the judge for a favorable decision. . . . Justice down here isn't merely blind . . . she also has a price tag.

Congress worked for Diaz, not for the voters. Every congressman was the president's tool, and Diaz often referred to the legislators as "my herd of tame horses." Church, courts, press, state governments, local officials, and police paid fealty to Diaz, not the people. He ruled the land with what an observer called the "most perfect one-man system on earth."

Further to safeguard his position, Diaz gave attractive inducements to foreign businessmen. He granted American and British speculators big concessions in the oil deposits along the Gulf coast. When an oil boom developed there, Mexico became one of the world's most important producers of petroleum.

Railroad builders were encouraged to put down thousands of miles of track at a handsome profit for every mile. Foreign investors raked in millions of dollars and shared this quick money with Mexican officials.

Despite the graft and corruption with which he was surrounded, El Presidente concentrated on bolstering his dictatorship and constantly spurned chances to make his own fortune. He tried to satisfy all foreigners, but lost favor among certain influential American financial manipulators when he gave British oil interests the inside track to supplies of oil. Angered by this British coup, American businessmen persuaded Washington to "put the screws" to Diaz. El Presidente never quite succeeded in erasing the mistrust of him north of the border.

Still, things were not too bad. Despite hard feelings, American investors continued to pour money into Mexico.

This flow of capital had a side effect. Even under Diaz, some benefits trickled down to the Mexican people. Foreigners grew so rich that many of them spent excess funds on philanthropic projects such as hospitals and schools. But this sort of charity did little to ease the deep poverty in which most Mexicans were doomed to live. Although Diaz treated his own people harshly, he accorded foreigners the fullest deference. The government's share of income from foreign-operated mines and oil wells was small. Oil developers paid no taxes, but the Mexican people were burdened with them. When necessary, laws were changed to benefit foreign investors.

The preferential treatment given aliens irked the proud and touchy Mexicans. Antiforeign incidents erupted and were promptly put down by Rurales, bravistas, and troops. As one observer put it:

> The emphasis on development and industrialization widened the already vast gulf between rich and poor in Mexico. . . . A handful tasted splendor and opulence, most were subjected to appalling hardships. Diaz did bring industry to his country . . . he did develop its natural resources—but he failed to develop the people, and what was worse, he simply did not care. Small wonder that the Mexicans felt that their country was a mother to foreigners and a stepmother to them.

Diaz could have done much for his people. He had the means to abolish illiteracy, to train skilled workers, and to establish a prosperous middle class. Instead he relied upon foreign technicians and forced his people into social, political, and economic servitude. The last thing he wanted was an enlightened citizenry capable of taking over and running the country in a democratic fashion. This did not jibe with Diaz's dream of gaining and keeping absolute power. That dream was the driving force of his life and he would let nothing keep him from realizing it.

- 3 -

HERITAGE OF HATRED

When Spain ruled Mexico, millions of Indians—who made up the bulk of the population—lived an independent existence, cultivating the commonly owned land of their small towns and villages. These tracts, known as *ejidos,* were divided up among the peasants, depending in size on the number in a family and the fertility of the soil. Naturally, those with larger families got more land. Each ejido shared pastureland and water rights with the rest.

But this primitive form of communism came to an end in 1856, when a law was passed to abolish communal property. Peasants were required to pay a small sum for their ejidos, which then became their private property. Not accustomed to individual ownership, the Indians did not know their rights and fell easy prey to land dealers.

Corrupt officials played along with the land sharks and advised the Indians that they must sell their holdings for whatever price was offered. In this way, smart operators assembled vast tracts along proposed rights-of-way for railroads, while the innocent Indians went on blithely sowing, reaping, and tilling land that no longer belonged to them.

18

When the railroads came through, the speculators sold their parcels for large sums and the new owners evicted the Indians. Baffled and bewildered, peasants who had been living on the land for hundreds of years were turned out. Wealthy *hacendados* created tremendous estates by taking over Indian holdings.

If a peasant resisted, he was arrested and a crooked judge either sent him off to the army for ten years or exiled him to slavery on some faraway plantation. Such men rarely saw their loved ones again. Left without alternatives, once-independent Indians went to work on the haciendas as peons, and were treated like serfs.

Typically, a hacendado did not even live on his estate. He usually left it in the hands of an overseer and spent his days in Mexico City, London, or Paris, leading a life of revelry, while his overseer mercilessly worked the peons on that portion of the hacienda being kept under cultivation.

Surrounding the luxurious estates were the dismal villages in which the peons lived. These unfortunates were in lifelong servitude to the hacendado. Each hacienda had a shop where the villagers were required to purchase all necessities. A peon received a tiny wage for his week's work, but was always in debt to the store and as a result never had any cash.

A peon's life was stringently regulated. He could not leave the land without paying off his debts to the store, and since he never had any money was bound for life to the hacienda. His children were similarly entrapped, for under Mexican law a child inherited the obligations of his parents.

Binding the peon to the hacienda even further was the fact that he was not paid in pesos, but in scrip that was worthless except at the hacienda's store. A peon had no legal rights. The manager of the store could charge him any price for such staples as milk, bread, eggs, and meat. These items were outrageously expensive, and no matter how hard or how long a peon worked he never could get out of debt.

"Peons have less value than a dog. I'd sooner shoot a peon than a dog. I can replace him more cheaply than I can the dog," a Yucatan plantation overseer once said. The subhuman conditions of their lives spawned in the peons a heritage of hatred for hacendados and those who served them. It was a bitter resentment passed on from father to son. This anger was masked by a veneer of meekness. Whenever the hacendado or an overseer approached, the peon would whip off his sombero and bow humbly. But under that facade of subservience seethed a hunger for revenge, a burning, tearing hunger that one day would erupt into unbridled fury.

Of Mexico's masses of downtrodden people, the Indians were by far the most oppressed. As one American resident put it: "To me all Mexicans—even the rich ones—are greasers. But the Indians are the niggers of Mexico."

Indians were humiliated in every way possible. Some towns and cities barred them from main streets and squares. When men were required for road building or other hard work, local police rounded up enough Indians to fill out the work gangs, arresting them on vague charges and putting them to toil on the roads. The police and the contractor split the money that should have gone to pay the wages of legitimate construction crews, and the hapless Indians sweated long hours under a blazing sun without getting a penny.

In some states, where Indians wore traditional garb —a loose white cotton shirt and baggy white cotton trousers like pajama bottoms—they had to rent European-type pants before entering town or else risk arrest.

The Indians as a whole accepted their lot. But not all of them knuckled under. Indian resistance to tyranny occurred in the state of Sonora, where the Yaqui tribe had owned land for centuries. Fierce and warlike, the Yaquis held onto their land even under the Spanish despite every effort to evict them. After several attempts to drive out the Yaquis, the Spanish had signed a treaty with them acknowledging their permanent right to the land. This treaty was honored by every ruler of Mexico until Diaz.

In the early 1880s, Diaz paid off a political debt to some Sonoran politicians by assigning certain Yaqui land to them. However, he was giving away property to which he had no title. The Yaquis refused to surrender their land. When Rurales came to evict them, the Indians, under the leadership of a chief named Cajeme, fought back.

This little war continued for some time. But in April 1887, Cajeme was captured and "shot while trying to escape." The next year, Diaz signed a peace pact with the Yaquis, who were forced onto a reservation far smaller and much less desirable than their former holdings. Even this was not enough for the land-grabbers. They tried to push the Yaquis off the new land and once again the long-suffering Indians had to take up arms.

They fought so hard that soldiers sent to put down the insurrection deserted by the score rather than do battle with the Yaquis. Diaz ordered ruthless tactics employed against the Indians. His close associate, Ramon Corral, the governor of Sonora, offered five hundred pesos to any soldier who killed a Yaqui and could prove it by bringing in the Indian's ears.

A great deal of bounty money was paid out, but this did not discourage the Yaquis from fighting harder than ever. Eventually, it was learned that the ears did not come from Yaqui warriors at all. The soldiers were murdering innocent peons and mutilating them for the bounty money.

As the war raged on, Diaz demanded total extermination of the Yaqui tribe. To carry out this genocide, soldiers and Rurales committed ghastly atrocities and wiped out whole communities. In May 1892, every man, woman, and child of Navojoa, a town in Sonora, was hanged because snipers had fired at soldiers from the town. So many went to the gallows that the supply of rope was exhausted and each piece had to be used several times. Another shocking massacre of Yaquis took place off the Pacific coast port of Guaymas, where two hundred Yaqui prisoners were taken out to sea in a gunboat and thrown overboard.

The end of the Yaqui war did not come until 1898, when the Mexican army, equipped with the latest German Mauser rifles, crushed a Yaqui force in a pitched battle near Mazacoba. Thousands of Indians capitulated after this defeat. Those who gave up were resettled on arid wasteland, a desert of rocks and waterless scorched earth, where nothing could be or ever had been grown.

Rather than go to this living hell, many Yaquis refused to stop fighting. They carried on guerrilla warfare from mountain caves. Diaz inflicted harsh punishment on these last-ditchers. He ordered wholesale deportations of their fathers, mothers, wives, children, and relatives. These unfortunates were rounded up like cattle and sold at three hundred pesos a head to owners of Yucatan hemp plantations.

There, in that tropical clime, the Yaquis died of fever, overwork, mistreatment, or heartbreak. Life no longer had meaning for them. This was tragically demonstrated in February 1908, when a shipload of Yaquis bound for Yucatan committed mass suicide by leaping into the sea.

The ship captain angrily told newsmen: "Those damned Indians cost me my commission money. . . . They threw all their youngsters overside and then jumped in after them. . . . Now, what the hell sort of people do a thing like that? Savages, I tell you! Dirty, filthy savages!"

A repressive government was not solely responsible for the miseries of Mexico's workers and peasants. During the later days of the Diaz regime inflation spread a blight over the nation. Everything rose in price. The spiraling cost of living sent the very necessities beyond the reach of the average Mexican. Within a few years, food, clothing, and shelter skyrocketed almost 400 percent without a rise in wages. With the cost of staples so high, slow starvation crept across the land. At the same time, the rich were getting richer. Foreigners tightened their grip on the economy. The gap between rich and poor grew ever wider.

The peons, even the Yaquis, posed no real threat to Diaz because they lacked unity and leadership. But El Presidente was endangered by a newly emerging force in Mexico—the industrial working class. In a sense, Diaz had sowed the seeds of his own destruction when he brought industry to the country.

He had intended to create a Garden of Eden for employers—a paradise where profits were high and wages low. The factory workers, oil riggers, miners, and other types of industrial labor recruited from city slums and impoverished farms were tractable at first, glad to earn even the most meager income on a regular basis. Before 1900, labor unions did not exist in Mexico and strikes were illegal.

But that began to change when Mexicans who had lived and worked in the United States came home. They had been made aware of the rights that labor was beginning to enjoy north of the border; they had been exposed to unions, decent working conditions, and good pay. Like missionaries, these returnees spread the gospel of organization among workers in the homeland. The Mexican workers were eager converts. They formed unions and raised demands for shorter hours, higher wages, and better conditions. The bosses responded by firing militant unionists. The battle was on.

The aroused workers could no longer be intimidated by their employers. An astute observer might have seen that capital and labor were on a collision course and taken measures to avert the catastrophe in the offing.

But astuteness was not common in Diaz's regime. Social problems were smashed, not solved. The men who ruled Mexico held workers in contempt as inferior beings. To employers, especially foreign ones, Mexican workers lacked both the brains and courage necessary for decisive action.

Precisely how wrong this appraisal was became apparent on June 1, 1906, when two thousand workers of an American-owned mining company in Cananea, Sonora, walked off the job. The main grievance was a difference in pay scale between Mexican and American workers doing the same jobs. The Mexicans demanded equal pay for equal work.

The company refused to deal with the strikers. Violence flared when a delegation of Mexicans marched to the company office and called on American workers to join the strike. The Americans replied with shotguns, rifles, and pistols. A riot followed as enraged strikers wrecked company property and fought with Americans.

Troops were rushed to the mine and martial law declared. The soldiers shot more than twenty strikers and many more were jailed. Bayonets and bullets finally broke the walkout, but the defeat at Cananea did not stifle rising labor discontent. More strikes, more disorders erupted. Unrest reached near-epidemic proportions. The discontent finally roused Diaz. He promised to investigate the workers' demands. Predictably, his decision favored the capitalists. According to him, labor had no just complaints about wages or working conditions.

This infuriated labor and caused serious trouble. When Diaz's findings were announced on January 7, 1907, textile workers in Veracruz rioted. The disorders spread through the city. Factories were set afire and the homes of millowners wrecked. Federal soldiers and Rurales mowed down workers in the streets. More than two hundred rioters were arrested and executed by firing squads.

An American eyewitness wrote: "This government has made Mexico safe for tourists and foreign businessmen . . . but plain Mexican citizens certainly have not benefited from the achievements of Porfirio Diaz and the killers he keeps to slaughter his own people."

After the Veracruz slayings, the strikes ended. But defeating the workers proved to be a Pyrrhic victory for Diaz. The vicious means he had used revealed him to Mexican workers as their enemy. This opened the door to revolution.

Diaz's acts had alienated the only group in Mexico strong enough to unseat him. In his early career he would have been politically aware enough to see the need for making an ally of labor. But Diaz had grown old. He chose to side with foreign businessmen, and this was his fatal error; he had sold out his own people for the blandishments of aliens. His usefulness to Mexico was coming to an end. In fact, El Presidente had become a relic. Mexico needed more than a dictator. She needed integrity, honesty, and above all freedom. Diaz could not provide any of these. The Veracruz incident was not the end of Diaz—but it marked the beginning of the end.

- 4 -

THE CIENTIFICOS

It seemed quite natural for a regime like Diaz's to formulate a high-flown philosophy to explain its excesses. Although Diaz rarely stopped to ponder the rights and wrongs of his conduct in office, there gathered about him a group of men who considered themselves deep thinkers and intellectuals.

This presidential clique was known as the *cientificos* —the scientific ones—despite the fact that not one was a scientist of any sort. The cientificos included business-men, bankers, politicians, and editors. What they had in common was total subservience to Diaz.

The founder of the cientificos was Diaz's father-in-law, Romero Rubio, a man whose scientific knowledge was limited to roulette wheels, poker, dice, and blackjack. Thanks to his son-in-law, the president, Rubio ran most of the gambling houses in Mexico City, a deal that made him a millionaire in a remarkably short time. He enlisted other men whose wealth dated from the time Diaz had taken office.

The purpose of the cientificos was to perpetuate Diaz in the presidency and to keep the money rolling in. To attain this goal, Rubio and his cronies served as an un-official advisory board for Diaz. The cientificos influenced him to abandon the liberal tendencies of his own past.

According to them, Mexico was a land unsuited for democracy, freedom, and equality. The very social struc-ture of the country was a permanent barrier to a dem-ocratic form of government. The masses were shiftless, illiterate, and unable to cope with freedom. The bulk of the people, the Indians, were inferior beings, the cientif-icos declared. No segment of the Mexican population was capable, except those of pure Spanish descent. However, the cientificos did not stress this point too much; Diaz was a *mestizo*—a half-breed—of mixed Spanish and In-dian blood.

Thus, the brunt of the cientifico argument was aimed at the Indians; after all, the president was an exception to the average half-caste. He acted like a *castellano*, a Spaniard, one of the elite who deserved to rule. With such flattery, they wooed Diaz away from his original desire to better the lot of the masses. They persuaded him that progress meant more mines, mills, industries, railroads, and shops; progress was wealth and had nothing to do with schools, hospitals, the elimination of slums, an upgraded standard of living for all Mexicans.

Shrewd as he was, Diaz proved unbelievably gullible when it came to the cientificos. He completely failed to comprehend their real intent; by controlling his moves, this handful of men became the actual power in the land. As Diaz aged and grew even less perceptive, he became a mere figurehead, the tool of the cientificos.

By 1910, Diaz was completely in their power. He depended on them for advice in all state matters. The cientificos cleverly enmeshed him in their web; they practically controlled the government while he lived, and planned carefully to take over entirely after his death.

At eighty, Diaz could not live much longer. The top group of cientificos—sixteen men—patiently awaited his death. They could afford to wait. More than 75 percent of all government employees, army and navy officers, senators and congressmen were under their influence. No important opposition existed, except for a handful of malcontents—or so they chose to believe.

Romero Rubio had died in 1895 and the man who succeeded him as the cientifico leader, Jose Yves Limantour, enjoyed national renown. As minister of finance, Limantour had put the Mexican budget on its feet. The country was solvent for the first time since independence.

Unlike most politicians of his time, Limantour sought public office for fame, not graft, although he was not above pilfering a bit now and then. Wealthy in his own right, he had inherited a fortune from his father. The elder Limantour had struck gold in California during the Gold Rush of 1849–50 and then made a second fortune speculating in Mexican real estate.

Diaz had leaned heavily on Limantour for years, secure in the knowledge that Limantour, while not above temptation, was more honest than the rest. During the later years of the Diaz regime, Limantour had a free hand and could spend public funds as he saw fit.

The minister of finance wanted to be remembered for the "improvements" he made in Mexico City. He was determined to have the national capital look like a carbon copy of Paris. As a result, ornate government buildings were put up. The monstrous National Theater was erected. People with taste detested the sprawling marble pile, which started sinking into Mexico City's marshy soil even before it was completed. Limantour also built the National Palace and other structures. He did give Mexico a superficial resemblance to Paris, but the Mexican capital lacked the grace and culture of the City of Light.

Nor could the fine buildings mask the slum areas where workers lived in filth and squalor unequaled almost anywhere in the world. Not a single piece of work by a native artist dressed the capital. When a new statue of Juarez was commissioned, Limantour had it done in France by an Italian sculptor who never had seen either Juarez or Mexico.

That statue offered a footnote to the Diaz dictatorship. Even the nation's foremost hero had been sold out to foreign interests.

RELUCTANT REVOLUTIONARY

Diaz had won the presidential election of 1896 easily. His only opponent was a harmless crackpot, Zuniga y Miranda, who wandered about in a frock coat and top hat making garbled speeches filled with predictions of catastrophes and doom—earthquakes, fires, floods, and plagues. Zuniga gave a comic touch to the campaign, and even Diaz's elite strong-arm squads, the bravistas, let him rant unhampered.

In 1900, the first presidential election of the twentieth century, Diaz enjoyed another overwhelming triumph. The outcome was a foregone conclusion. But the election was marred by a macabre occurrence that took place during the six-hour-long victory parade. A beautiful girl, chosen parade queen, was tied in place high on a float atop a huge plaster cast statue of Diaz.

The day was exceptionally hot and the queen stood exposed to the sun for hours. Not until the parade's end did anyone notice that the girl was dead of sunstroke. Incredibly, she had remained smilingly erect, eyes open, an arm raised in greeting to the onlookers. Noting the incident, a Mexico City newspaper remarked: "El Presidente's admirers serve him with a devotion stronger than life itself . . . even in death, they serve."

At the turn of the century, Diaz was seventy years old. His advancing years stirred speculation about his successor. Not that anyone actually expected him to die very soon. Diaz seemed almost immortal. Indeed, a music hall comedian always evoked laughter when he quipped, "Don Porfirio die? Ridiculous! Why, he'll simply pick up a pen and scribble a decree authorizing him to live for another fifty years!"

Despite El Presidente's longevity, certain influential men were busy behind the scenes seeking the right man to follow him. The cientificos touted their leader, Jose Limantour, but, for some obscure reason, the financial wizard had fallen somewhat in Diaz's estimation. The grizzled president had his own protégé, General Bernardo Reyes, the civil governor of Nuevo Leon state in northern Mexico and military commander of the northeast. Reyes had gone far under Diaz. He received a double salary as civil governor and military commander. The War Department provided him with ten thousand pesos per month for expenses, and he got his cut of an annual military budget that ran into a million pesos or better.

Pompous, fully bearded, Reyes wore a specially designed uniform in which he loved to be photographed. A dandy, he had bells on his spurs, a gold-tasseled sword, braided epaulets, and a wide sombrero from which golden bells dangled.

"When Reyes walked, he clanked, tinkled, and jangled, for all the world like a one-man band," an American reporter wrote.

Despite his appearance, the general did his job well. He crushed anti-Diaz demonstrations in Neuvo Leon with bayonets, cannon, and machine guns. But he was not all tyrant, displaying a surprising social consciousness at times and much compassion for poverty-stricken peons and workers. During his administration, Nuevo Leon established the first workmen's compensation law in Mexico. Reyes also initiated public health services and free public schools. He helped create jobs by pushing the development and industrialization of the city of Monterrey.

Reyes was extremely popular in the army and enjoyed the almost unanimous support of the officer corps. The general burned with aspiration for the presidency and did all he could to further that aim. One of his shrewdest moves was to latch onto Diaz. He became an ardent supporter of the president and was rewarded in 1900 by an appointment as minister of war in the cabinet.

The cientificos were against Reyes, though. They wanted a businessman, not a soldier, to follow Diaz. Those close to the president continued to advocate Limantour and gradually managed to move Diaz away from Reyes and back to their man. Then El Presidente suddenly turned on Reyes, kicked him out of the cabinet, and sent him off to Nuevo Leon, where the crestfallen general had time to mull over the fickleness of politicians.

When 1904 rolled around, Diaz admitted that the years were catching up to him. "No man lasts forever and I am no exception," he said. Thus, once again returned to the presidency, Diaz announced that now he agreed to the appointment of a vice-president. His only condition was that he must choose the man. At the same time, he quietly issued a decree extending the president's term from four years to six years.

With a vice-presidential appointment in the offing, both the Limantour and the Reyes factions took fresh hope. Reyes again had been reinstated in Diaz's favor after his dismissal from the cabinet. But the president also kept the cientificos happy by his attentions to Limantour. None seemed to be aware that Diaz was at his old game of promising everybody everything and delivering nothing.

He showed his hand at a convention held just prior to the 1904 elections. Reyes and Limantour supporters gathered in a Mexico City auditorium to await Diaz's selection of the vice-president. El Presidente enjoyed himself by keeping the delegates in suspense until the closing hours of the convention. A messenger, bringing the name of the vice-president, came dashing into the hall.

An astonished gasp went up from the assemblage when the choice was made public. He was Ramon Corral, now the minister of the interior, an unsavory man who had made his fortune as a Yaqui slave trader.

The fifty-year-old minister was notorious in Mexico City for the dissolute life he led. Except for fanatical loyalty to Diaz, Corral had little to qualify him as vice-president. Singularly unpopular, he was known as "Butcher" Corral because as governor of Sonora during a Yaqui uprising twenty-five years before he ordered a massacre of Indians after they had surrendered. He was disliked by workers and peons; fellow politicians were contemptuous of him. Seldom in any country had such a universally detested man risen to high office.

Observers of the Mexican political scene soon deduced why Diaz had picked Corral. The wily old president had tapped his minister of the interior precisely because of Corral's unpopularity. With him as vice-president, it was unlikely that anyone would assassinate Diaz to make Corral president.

"Hardly ever did Diaz make a move without a damned good reason," an American resident of Mexico City said. "He might have slipped a bit by 1904, but the choice of Corral was shrewd enough."

The furor over the vice-president soon died away. Like other Diaz aides, Corral sank into almost complete obscurity. He had few duties as vice-president and served as a ceremonial figure at events that Diaz found too boring or tiring. Corral understood his role and once told a visitor, "Porfirio remembers me only when he wants me to attend some official function not convenient for him. The day is hot, raining, cold, let Ramon go!"

During his final years in office, Diaz became openly resentful of the vast American commercial interests in Mexico. United States businessmen had siphoned billions of dollars into the country and Diaz began to worry that American investors would foment a revolution to gain control of Mexico.

In order to counteract top-heavy American financial and commercial involvements, Diaz encouraged other foreign businesses to put their money in Mexico. He offered wide tax concessions to British, French, German, and Japanese speculators. By 1909, Mexico was host to commercial missions from those nations. While Americans still had the most in the pot, their lead had been cut quite a bit.

This influx of foreign business into Mexico irked the Americans. Certain influential men arranged a goodwill meeting between the American president, William Howard Taft, and Diaz. The main reason for this conference, at El Paso, Texas, was to assure United States oilmen of important franchises and leaseholds on potential sources of oil along the Gulf of Mexico.

Diaz held his answer in abeyance. He promised to let Taft know in the near future. A second reason for the El Paso meeting was the United States request for renewal of a lease on Magdalena Bay in Lower California. For some years, this site had served the U.S. Pacific Fleet as a coaling and repair station.

Taft had no doubt that the lease would be renewed without any problem. Magdalena Bay played an important part in United States naval strategy in the Pacific. It was particularly needed in view of Japan's rising aggressiveness after her defeat of Russia in the Russo-Japanese War of 1904–05.

Sensationalist American newspapers were playing up the so-called Yellow Peril as exemplified by Japan. It was assumed that Diaz went along with Washington's policy of containing Japan—by force, if necessary. However, El Presidente had decided to harpoon the United States and promptly did so by rejecting Taft's request for a long-term occupation of Magdalena Bay. Taft stomped away from El Paso seething with anger. Diaz was delighted by the American's discomfiture.

El Presidente further irked Washington by throwing a reception in Mexico City for a group of touring Japanese marines. At a banquet honoring the Oriental guests, Admiral Isoruku Yashiro, grand admiral of the Imperial Japanese Navy, delivered a saber-rattling speech in which he strongly hinted at joint action by Japan and Mexico against the United States. Yashiro's anti-American tirade was greeted by shouts of *"Abajos los gringos!"*—"Down with the gringos!"

Diaz felt secure in tweaking Uncle Sam's nose. Neither he nor those around him were aware that El Presidente was approaching the end of the line. The closing act of the Diaz regime came without fanfare.

In 1908, El Presidente himself gave his foes the opening they needed by revealing in a magazine interview that he would not stand for reelection in 1910. He told the reporter: "Regardless of the feelings and opinions of my friends and supporters, I am determined to retire at the end of my present term and will not accept reelection. . . ."

When the story broke in a New York City magazine, it was picked up and translated by daily papers in Mexico. The reaction to the piece was quite the opposite of what Diaz had anticipated. He had expected mass protest against his retirement.

When Diaz saw that no popular clamor for him to reconsider was developing, he backtracked. A few weeks after proclaiming the forthcoming retirement, Diaz told the country he had been "persuaded" to stand again in 1910, "for the good of the nation."

However, a political grab bag of anti-Diazistas resolved to run a candidate in the 1910 election. They cast about for the proper man. He had to be from a respectable family of some wealth. Their aspirant must be well educated, although not necessarily politically known. He

had to be a liberal, but he was required to have conservative ties. Above all, he had to be a man of talent,
skill, courage, and the capability of reaching men's hearts
and minds.

Finding the ideal man was no easy matter, but someone close to him actually turned up. He was Francisco
Indalecio Madero, a thirty-seven-year-old hacendado
from Coahuila. A singularly unimpressive-looking young
man, Madero stood only five feet two inches tall. Frail in
health and delicate in physique, he wore a goatee to hide
a receding chin. With thinning hair and a high-pitched
voice that sometimes broke in a falsetto squeak, Madero
seemed an unlikely choice. He certainly could rouse no
public support on his appearance alone.

But, lacking physical attractiveness, Madero had
something more. He was courageous and fired by a burning zeal to save his beloved country from the Diaz dictatorship. The sincerity of his dedication to freedom,
democracy, and equality inspired many others to believe
as he did.

Although Madero seemed to pose no threat to Diaz,
he had the brains and the ambition to do the job. Born
in 1873, Francisco Madero was the eldest child of one
of the richest landowning families of northern Mexico.
The Maderos—of Portuguese and Jewish stock—were not
involved in politics as were many hacendados. Their energies went into enlarging the family fortune, which had
been started by Francisco's grandfather, Don Evaristo
Madero.

The Madero clan owned vast land tracts, mines,
mills, factories, and wineries. When Don Evaristo died
in April 1911, at the age of eighty-two, he left behind
fourteen children, thirty-four grandchildren, fifty-six
great-grandchildren, and more than two million acres of
real estate. His actual cash worth was incalculable.

Young Francisco Indalecio Madero led a privileged
life of wealth. Privately tutored for a time, he later at-

tended schools in Mexico, the United States, and France. His stays abroad deeply impressed him. For in France and north of the border he saw democracy at work, and preferred it to what he had known in Mexico under Diaz.

Francisco's affinity for democracy was shared by his young brother, Gustavo. After five years out of the country, Francisco returned to the family hacienda and was placed in charge of certain family holdings. Given a free hand, he improved conditions for his workers, much to the annoyance of neighboring landowners. He paid higher wages, provided his people with good housing, and built schools on his estates. He hired the teachers, paying their salaries out of his own pocket since the government refused to help him in this educational project. Madero gladly spent the money, for he firmly believed that only mass education could bring progress to Mexico.

In 1904, breaking with family tradition, Madero participated in politics by founding the Club Democratico Benito Juarez, a reform movement aimed at bringing democracy to Mexico. Francisco labored day and night for the club, writing leaflets and pamphlets explaining democracy to the people. He made speeches to listless audiences. Had he not been so rich and influential, people probably would not have paid any attention to him. But they did notice the frail little man, whom one foreign newspaperman characterized as "a Mexican Don Quixote . . . embarked on a noble quest . . . to slay the dragon Diaz." Another journalist likened him to a hunter "with a peashooter trying to bring down a rhinoceros."

Perhaps Madero might have spent his years vainly preaching about the benefits of a democratic society to unheeding men, but help came from an unexpected source, Diaz himself. When Diaz changed his mind and decided to run again, he became vulnerable to attack. Madero was the one man with enough nerve to lambaste El Presidente. He did not unleash a furious assault; on the contrary, Francisco's onslaught was on a lofty and intellectual plane—he wrote a book bearing the mundane title *The Presidential Succession of 1910,* a tome which hardly seemed to pack dynamite. Yet this work changed the course of Mexican history, although its contents dealt, in a dull and scholarly manner, with the country's political condition. At no point in the book did Madero so much as mention Mexico's economic shortcomings, even though he was quite aware of them.

The Presidential Succession of 1910 exploded on the country with the impact of a blockbuster. After he had droned on for pages and pages, Madero finally got to the nub of things—the need for a change. On this subject, he was like a skillful boxer, stinging with rapierlike jabs, stunning with powerhouse blows.

All Madero's idealism and dedication went into that scathing critique of the Diaz regime. Nowhere did he make a personal reference to El Presidente, but he mercilessly flayed the Diaz dictatorship. He cried out over and over again for full freedom of suffrage and demanded a finish to the policy of reelection that permitted one man to hold office as long as he chose to continue—or as long as he could stifle opposition.

Madero did not advocate revolution to bring about change; instead he called for "peaceful reform." He was so worried about being tarred with the brush of revolution that he had delayed publication of the book until the Madero clan agreed to allow it to come out. Francisco was concerned that the book might adversely affect the family's enterprises, but when the family elders gave him the green light, the manuscript was rushed to the printer. The Madero family would have preferred that Francisco not engage in politics, but he was old enough to do what he wanted and they let him do it.

The Presidential Succession of 1910 came off the presses in January 1909. A first edition of three thousand copies went to bookstores and dealers. One of the first books was sent for comment to El Presidente. Apparently

what Diaz had to say was hardly complimentary, for
Madero never revealed the president's reactions to the
book.

But there was no doubt how the general public felt
about it. The first printing disappeared in a twinkling
and more editions were dispatched to bookstores. Over-
night, Madero was catapulted into the limelight; he was
the hero of the previously silent anti-Diaz factions.

Here was a man who had the courage to put in print
sharp criticisms of the dictatorship. No matter that
Madero reaffirmed his loyalty to Diaz. At least he had
rapped the system. For Mexico, in 1909, this was a sensa-
tional departure from the cowed acceptance most Mexicans rendered the regime.

By publishing the book, Madero gave up all his alternatives. Once the book appeared there was no turning
back for him. Willingly or not, he was the voice of dissent
in Mexico.

Madero, who had denounced revolution, was fated
to lead one, for his pen had unleashed a revolutionary tide
that would inflict on Mexico a decade of cruel war, bloodshed, and terror.

- 6 -

THE PLAN OF SAN LUIS POTOSI

Madero's book fueled the fires of discord. Not for
years had there been so much political activity as that
which took place in 1909, especially after the president

announced that he was offering the country another Diaz-Corral ticket in 1910.

No serious opposition to Diaz had existed since he first took office. But it developed in 1909. The new political organization was called the Anti-Reelectionist party. It was founded by fifty Mexican professional men—doctors, lawyers, teachers, artists, writers, and editors. The party had no program beyond opposition to another term for Diaz.

Madero was made the party's leader for several reasons. Few Mexicans of any status dared oppose Diaz for fear of reprisals. El Presidente had ruined more than one man who displeased him; prosperous business people suddenly found themselves bankrupt and ostracized by former associates; doctors lost their practices; lawyers were no longer retained by clients. Diaz only had to let the word out and his victim was doomed.

In all Mexico, Madero was almost the only well-known person who had enough money and position to defy even Diaz. The Madero family was too big, too important for the president to take on. And because of his personal wealth, Francisco could afford to spend his full time on politics.

As in the past, Diaz took steps to assure his victory at the polls in 1910. He dismissed the Anti-Reelectionists and concentrated on those he considered to be more of a threat. El Presidente did not doubt that he would win hands down, but the possibility of Corral's being defeated was a real one. (At that time, in Mexico, the people voted separately for the president and vice-president.)

Obviously, no one was going to pit himself against Diaz; but there were men ready to try for the second place. For a while, the leading contender was Jose Limantour, the darling of the cientificos. But Limantour decided that the reward was not worth the effort and turned down all offers to run for vice-president. Thus, the race narrowed down to Diaz's handpicked man, Ramon

Corral, and the army's hopeful, General Bernardo Reyes. The Anti-Reelectionists also made public the news that they would have an aspirant for the position.

Don Porfirio ignored the Antis, but worried about Reyes. The general had the army's backing and if elected vice-president might well use his influence with the armed forces to overthrow the regime and take power himself.

El Presidente decided to eliminate the Reyes threat. He removed the general from his command in the northeast, replacing him with a longtime Diaz sycophant, General Jacinto Trevino. When Reyes was summarily relieved, many officers urged him to rise against Diaz, but the general lost his nerve, retired to his hacienda, and announced that he would support Corral.

However, Diaz was not quite through. He stripped Reyes of the Nuevo Leon governorship and then sent the unhappy general on a military mission that required travel to a number of European countries. It was a neat way to keep Reyes out of the country until after the election.

Had Reyes been a resolute man of high principles, he would have disobeyed his orders and led a military coup against Diaz. It would have had more than an even chance of success. Instead, he meekly obeyed El Presidente and sailed for Europe from Veracruz in October 1909.

"They've put Bernardo on ice. If only he had guts, the army would be running things," a ranking officer complained.

Now the track was cleared for Diaz and Corral. The only cloud was the vociferous opposition of the Anti-Reelectionists. Diaz was assured that the Antis didn't amount to anything. But when speakers from a pro-Diaz group set out to stump the country, they were stoned and driven out of town by irate peons and workers in Guadalajara and Guanajuato. Insulated in the National Palace, Diaz refused to recognize the importance of these demonstrations and he put the disorders down to "malcontents, drunkards, and misfits."

Madero undertook a speaking tour. He had openly proclaimed himself in opposition to the regime and all it stood for. The receptions accorded him contrasted sharply with those given the Diaz crowd. People hailed Madero with wild enthusiasm. In some places he was carried on the shoulders of the spectators and paraded through the streets. Pretty girls showered him with flowers and kisses. Men wrung his hand. Everywhere he went, the frail man was hailed as a savior.

No spellbinder as a speechmaker, Madero roused audiences with his logic and sheer grit. His trip awakened Mexico from political torpor. New supporters flocked to him from every side. Many former Reyes backers joined him, not so much out of any belief in Madero, but to strike back at Diaz. By the time Madero had completed his rounds, an active opposition was working against Diaz, Corral, the cientificos, and all the old clique.

At last, Madero's successes made Diaz see that countermeasures had to be taken. The amused tolerance with which he had regarded Madero turned to wrath. At an order from Diaz, bravi toughs swung into action. Madero meetings were broken up. Hotels refused to rent rooms to Maderistas. Mayors of towns and cities where rallies were scheduled for Madero barred him from speaking within city limits. Madero soon found himself talking in sparsely populated areas to small crowds because so many people feared to come hear him.

The repressive tactics of the government scared off many Anti-Reelection party members. Battling ill health, Madero strove hard all winter long to keep the party alive. His efforts paid off and when spring rolled around again the Antis were still in business.

On April 15, 1910, the party held its first convention, in Mexico City, to choose a presidential candidate and his running mate. There was no point in fielding only a vice-presidential aspirant. If Diaz won, he would accept no one the Antis put up, anyway.

The regime made every effort to sabotage the convention. Vice-President Corral signed a warrant for Madero's arrest on charges of subversion. To this Madero replied, "I call upon you to come down to our convention hall and arrest me!" This Corral hesitated to do. He knew that any attempt to put Madero in custody would cause bloodshed, for many Maderistas showed up at the hall carrying rifles and pistols.

The Anti-Reelectionist convention went off without a hitch. Madero was unanimously nominated for the presidency, while Dr. Francisco Vasquez Gomez, once Diaz's personal physician, was the vice-presidential nominee.

Diaz heard the news and sent for Madero to assure him that the election would be "free and fair." This so touched Madero that he told Diaz, "I hold you in high personal esteem. I must repeat . . . I am not opposing you personally but the system you represent. Mexico has had enough of dictatorship. To flourish, she must have an era of democracy. . . . For the sake of the Republic, you must relinquish your power."

El Presidente nodded sagely. "I see. And to whom shall I pass the power? Into whose hands?"

"Into the hands of an honest man," Madero replied.

"An honest man? *An honest man?*" Diaz chuckled. "My dear Madero, it will take more than an honest man to govern Mexico. Honesty is the least of his requirements!"

The interview soon ended. Neither man seemed to have made much of an impression on the other. Diaz told an aide, "Madero is another *loco* like Zuniga y Miranda. But this one prattles about democracy and freedom as though Mexicans would know what to do with such concepts."

44

Madero had little to say about Diaz except: "The old man cares nothing about the country. He cares only about himself . . . not what is good for the country, but what is good for Porfirio."

For a time it appeared as though Diaz meant to keep his promise of a free and fair election. Madero and other Anti speakers addressed large crowds in Puebla and Guadalajara. No one interfered with their meetings or hampered their movements. But this idyll lasted only a few weeks.

Diaz was angered because Madero was drawing large crowds. It rankled to know that so many Mexicans no longer trusted him. El Presidente decided to stop his rival while he still could.

The first blow fell in June when Madero and a fellow Anti, Roque Estrada, came to Monterrey for a political rally. A big crowd waited to greet Madero at the railroad station. But this gathering was dispersed by mounted police and cavalry troopers who used clubs, gun butts, and sabers to break up the peaceful assemblage.

Despite the violence unleashed against them, the people regrouped to hear Madero speak from the balcony of a house in Monterrey. The police and soldiers permitted him to deliver a brief speech, but Estrada was arrested when he tried to speak. As Madero argued with the arresting officers, Estrada managed to get away. The police then took Madero into custody for "aiding and abetting" Estrada's escape.

When he heard that Madero was being held, Estrada surrendered himself. Both men were detained on charges of inciting rebellion. They remained in prison until after the June 26 election.

The election was a farce. Police, soldiers, bravis, Rurales, and plain hoodlums so terrorized voters that most stayed clear of polling places. Only dyed-in-the-wool Diazistas were allowed free access to voting booths.

On July 10, to nobody's surprise, the Electoral Col-

45

lege announced that the Diaz-Corral ticket had won resoundingly. Ten days later Madero and Estrada were released from jail, but had to remain under strict police surveillance while awaiting trial in San Luis Potosi.

Madero protested the election results. His cries of fraud were justified. According to the Electoral College, he had received only 196 votes in all of Mexico.

"Our politicos could learn a few tricks down Mexico way," wrote a New York City reporter covering the campaign. "When it comes to rigging elections Don Porfirio leads the pack!"

Madero's complaints were disregarded. Actually, few Mexicans became very upset over Diaz's tainted triumph. Even if mass protest had been aroused, it would have been lost in the excitement of the forthcoming festivities in September.

It seemed that only Madero and a few devoted followers cared about the country's fate under another Diaz term. Sadly and reluctantly, Madero came to realize that the only way to get rid of Diaz was with force—a prospect that went against his nature. But after much self-probing and introspection, Madero decided that Mexico was more important than his repugnance to violence.

Although lacking men and weapons, Madero decided to head an insurrection against the regime. At the time he could count only on his brothers—Gustavo, Raul, Alfonso, and Julio—and his old friend Estrada. But in the past revolutions had been launched by fewer men than that. The only requirements were a leader and a just cause; in Mexico, it was not hard to round up men for a fight.

Madero sneaked out of San Luis Potosi on October 6, 1910, and boarded a Texas-bound train. He took lodgings in a small San Antonio hotel where Estrada and his brothers joined him. As word of Madero's intentions leaked back into Mexico, small groups of men drifted across the border to reinforce the anti-Diaz conspirators.

After some fifty or so men had rallied to him, Madero proclaimed himself the provisional president of a revolutionary government and sent out a call for a revolt against Diaz.

It was traditional for the leader of a Mexican insurrection to publish a political "plan" or statement of his aims. In it he would carefully detail the course to be taken once the people had helped him obtain power. So Madero issued the Plan of San Luis Potosi. Under it, the recent elections were to be nullified and free elections held as soon as the country was taken over by the "people." All laws and decrees enacted during Diaz's long reign would be reviewed and revised. Certain land reforms would be enacted.

Printed copies of the Plan were smuggled into Mexico and distributed on haciendas, in army barracks, among trade unionists and peons. Madero and his colleagues then got busy planning an uprising to begin at midnight, Saturday, November 19, 1910.

After thirty years, Diaz was faced with the reality he had always dreaded. The banner of revolt was raised in Mexico. *La Revolución* was at hand.

- 7 -

"VIVA LA REVOLUCION!"

What was to become the first great social upheaval of the twentieth century started off badly and clumsily. Even by the comic opera standards that had marked past Mexican rebellions, this one reached new highs—or lows.

From the outset there was a good deal of amateurish bungling by the rebels. No sooner did Diaz get hold of a copy of the Plan of San Luis Potosi than he began to take countersteps with professional skill.

He immediately lodged a protest with Washington over the presence on American soil of Madero and his comrades. Diaz charged the United States with harboring rebels plotting to overthrow the government of a friendly nation. He demanded that Madero be expelled from the United States.

The American government complied. Madero and the rest were warned to clear out in forty-eight hours on pain of arrest and imprisonment. Even as this order was given, Madero was handing out cash to American arms dealers for guns and ammunition.

On the Mexican side of the Rio Grande, Diaz's police had been rounding up suspected Maderistas. Kangaroo courts passed death sentences on the spot and firing squads worked overtime. Tensions grew and on November 18, the day before the Revolution was supposed to start, sharp fighting broke out between Maderistas and federal soldiers at Puebla, many miles south of the Texas border. The overeager revolutionaries attacked the local garrison, and a hot gun battle ensued. Participants on both sides were killed and wounded. The wild fray ended with the rebels giving up. Again the execution squads went into action.

The news from Puebla depressed Madero; the situation was bad enough without such tidings. When his forty-eight hours were up, Madero left San Antonio. He offered a singularly unprepossessing appearance as he crossed the Rio Grande into his native land. Mounted on a big, rawboned horse, he looked wizened and undersized. A big pistol strapped to his waist flopped around in its holster; the gun belt sagged low because it was too large for his small waistline. He blinked nearsightedly through scholarly pince-nez glasses, more like a myopic philosophy professor than the leader of a revolution.

Like a crusading knight, Madero splashed across the shallow Rio Grande surrounded by his few followers. On the Mexican side of the border, he was supposed to rendezvous with some three hundred men commanded by one of his relatives. The objective of this force was to be Piedras Negras, a border town. Once it was captured, Madero would have a foothold in Mexican territory that could serve as a base from which to press the Revolution.

Alas for Madero's high hopes. His party got lost in the darkness and missed the rendezvous. As a result, Madero spent his first night as provisional president of Mexico in an Indian shack near the border.

La Revolucion was meant to start that midnight. It was to have been Madero's hour of glory as he gave the signal for his followers to rise up in factories, mines, mills, fields, and barracks. Instead, he shared his bed of flea-infested straw with the Indian's pigs and chickens.

Sunday, November 20, dawned dull and dreary. It was a day for gloomy thoughts and Madero had a lot of them. Not only had he not made contact with his "army," but also a shipment of arms, which he had paid for in advance, had not been hauled to the Mexican side of the river as arranged.

To make matters even more dismal, when the missing "army" turned up it numbered not three hundred men but only ten—poorly armed at that. The provisional president eyed the sorry-looking bunch and muttered, "Somebody doesn't know how to count."

Unhappily, Madero retraced his steps back over the Rio Grande, believing that his Revolution had flopped before it began.

Diaz must have come to the same conclusion. He issued a glowing statement to the press, saying in part:

> The political situation in Mexico does not pre-
> sent any danger . . . the lives and interests of all
> foreigners are absolutely secure. All that has
> occurred to disturb order is a few mutinies of
> small importance. . . . These have been sup-
> pressed.

However, El Presidente was a bit too optimistic. The
fires of Madero's Revolution were far from extinguished.
They were rekindled in the poverty-stricken, barren north
of Mexico where the people endured such abject misery
that not even life had any worth. Men who knew nothing
but oppression would dare any peril to get some promise
of rising from the dark pit of their unhappy existence.

The downtrodden Mexicans of the north came to
Madero's rescue. They made La Revolucion and they won
it. They fought, bled, and died shouting, *"Viva la Revolución!*—Long Live the Revolution!" Leaders rose from
among them. One was Pascual Orozco, a tall, gaunt, blue-
eyed mountaineer of American and Mexican stock. Orozco,
who had been a freight handler, mule skinner, laborer,
and storekeeper, showed an unusual talent for warfare
and became a general in the ranks of the revolutionary
army.

Another rebel leader bore the unlikely name of
Doroteo Arango. He had been born into peonage on a
Durango hacienda in 1877, the year after Diaz assumed
power. When the hacendado's son raped young Arango's
sister, Doroteo avenged her honor by killing the man.
Forced to flee, Arango joined an outlaw band in the
Durango mountains and changed his name to Francisco
"Pancho" Villa.

As Pancho Villa, he went on to widespread notoriety.
Common people saw him as a sort of Robin Hood who
took from the rich and gave to the poor. He championed
the oppressed and they admired him for his daring crimes
against the wealthy. But even though Villa was hailed

for his generosity to the peons, for his dash and courage, he was equally feared for his uncontrollable temper and incredible cruelty.

A man of medium height, Villa was strongly built. He walked at an ungainly gait on short, bowed legs. But on a horse Villa rode with grace and style. He had a thick, drooping moustache, which was imitated by young men who fancied themselves to be his counterparts.

Before Madero's Revolution started, Orozco, Villa, and others—labeled as "bandits" by the government—were already in arms against Diaz. Villa and Orozco were recruited for La Revolucion by a leading Chihuahua politician, Abraham Gonzalez, an ardent Anti-Reelectionist. Gonzalez gave each man some money and the rank of colonel in the as yet nonexistent Army of the Revolution.

Proudly wearing officers' swords, Orozco and Villa rode out to gather recruits for the cause. But even as Madero's forces were grouping, Diaz officially announced that the Revolution had fizzled out. Henry Lane Wilson, the United States ambassador to Mexico and an unabashed admirer of Diaz, cabled Washington: "The conspiracy lacks coherence and the government will easily suppress it. . . . There is a great lack of intelligent leadership amongst the so-called revolutionaries. . . ."

It was universally believed by foreign journalists in Mexico City that Diaz was firmly entrenched in office. One reporter wrote: "He has done his work well. . . . All the thousand productive results of continued peace have made civil war unattractive. . . . The Mexican people are too busy to fight each other now."

This contention seemed to be borne out for a while. The revolutionary leaders were despondent. Madero had spent thousands of pesos and even his substantial funds were almost depleted. In San Antonio, he and his comrades were reduced to eating only one meal a day.

Madero should have had faith in the revolutionary ardor of the Mexican people. Pancho Villa had recruited

51

a hard-riding band of some five hundred men. Under the banner of the Revolution, he captured a town in northern Chihuahua state. Orozco stormed and took the city of Guerrero in the southern part of the state. Although the rebels lacked both firepower and manpower to hold a populated area for any length of time, the fury of their attacks encouraged other uprisings.

A rebellion under a man named Jose Mantorena broke out in Sonora state, where a dozen rebel groups soon mushroomed. Guillermo Maca, a rich hacendado whose sympathies were with the people, joined a miner named Maclovio Herrera to capture the important mining town of Parral in Sonora.

At the same time, uprisings spread to Laguna, a cotton-growing region. Then the unrest jumped to Morelos, a state close to Mexico City. Prominent in the Morelos trouble was Margarita Neri, a fiery redheaded dancer. This hot-eyed beauty had once been a favorite of the Diaz inner circle. For some unexplained reason, Senorita Neri broke with the Diaz clique, took to the mountains, and formed her own bandit band. She was armed with a razor-sharp machete and swore to chop off Diaz's head with it.

After interviewing La Neri, an American newsman declared, "I don't know why she's so mad at Diaz, but now I believe that old saying about Hell having no fury like a woman scorned!"

8

"LAND AND LIBERTY!"

Margarita Neri probably was the most colorful of the revolutionaries. She had both beauty and passion and made good newspaper copy. Reporters sent back many stories about the "Rebel Queen of Morelos." In the United States, readers avidly devoured the deeds, real or imaginary, of the redheaded dancer turned rebel.

But despite all the interest shown in Senorita Neri, she was not the leader of the Morelos rebellion. The outstanding figure of the Revolution there was a small, slender young man named Emiliano Zapata.

He had singularly Asiatic features for a pure-blooded Mexican and they were emphasized by the Mandarin-style moustache he favored. Zapata's eyes were remarkably dark and piercing. An observer remarked about them: "When Zapata first fixed his gaze on one, the eyes were hard and cold; a glance to curdle one's blood. . . . But once he knew and trusted a man, those same merciless eyes twinkled with warmth and good humor."

Unlike Villa, who dressed and behaved roughly, Zapata was something of a dandy. He always wore somber black; a tight-fitting jacket; a huge, silver-studded sombrero. His manner was courtly. He had a taste for French wines, Arabian horses, and beautiful women of any nationality.

Born at the Morelos village of Anenecuilco, Zapata

was thirty-three years old in 1910. His family had been important in the village for decades. Unlike their fellow villagers, the Zapatas were not merely peons laboring on the local hacienda, which was owned by Don Ignacio de la Torre y Mier, President Diaz's son-in-law. The Zapatas were what was known as *medieros*—a step above peons. They cultivated land on a partnership basis with Don Ignacio.

This was a practice common among hacendados, who allotted certain acreage to peons and shared the profits from the crops with them. The principle behind this scheme was that medieros, having a stake in the crop, would work harder to cultivate their "own" land.

Emiliano and his brother, Eufemio, had inherited from their parents the whitewashed adobe and stone house that marked them as successful medieros who lived, ate, and dressed better than ordinary peons.

For some years, Emiliano and Eufemio had worked together raising melons. The brothers had saved the accrued profits and, in comparison to most of Anenecuilco, were quite well off. The money and status brought the Zapata brothers as close to independence as was possible for a Mexican of humble birth to reach in those days.

Soon after reaching manhood, Eufemio took his share of the money and went off to Veracruz, where he set up a peddler's route, going from place to place hawking pots, pans, needles, thread, pins, anything and everything he could sell.

Emiliano stayed in the village. He added to his income by trading horses on a small scale. A splendid rider, he became a figure familiar to all, galloping through the dusty village mounted on a spirited horse, booted and spurred "like a gentleman."

Emiliano had attracted attention even as a youth. He gained repute throughout Morelos and in Mexico City as a clever horse dealer and one of the best horse trainers about. Hacendados vied for his services and were willing to pay him well. But even though he prospered, dressed well, and had a silver-embossed saddle, the people of Anenecuilco and such surrounding hamlets as Villa de Ayala always considered him one of their own.

Anenecuilcanos thought so highly of Emiliano that they made him president of the village council, the youngest man ever to hold that post. They chose him, secure in the knowledge that Zapata would fight for their rights and that the hacendados could not bribe him as they had been able to do with council leaders in the past.

Emiliano proved this when Don Ignacio hired him, at a good salary, to run his stables in Mexico City, where he kept a string of superb Arabian horses. Zapata could have had a good thing for himself as overseer of Don Ignacio's stables. He would have been able to curry favor with his employer's friends and guests, ingratiating himself with rich and influential people.

There were opportunities for kickbacks and graft from feed merchants, blacksmiths, saddlers, and veterinarians who were eager for exclusive contracts in Don Ignacio's stable, the finest in all Mexico City.

But Emiliano was not a man to bow, wheedle, and make deals. The stay in the capital embittered him. He came home angered that Don Ignacio's horses lived in stalls more comfortable than the squalid huts of Anenecuilco. He vowed to change that. "Men are better than horses. They should live like men, not lower than animals," he declared.

As president of Anenecuilco's village council, he presented the villagers' grievances to Don Ignacio. But, unlike past council heads, he would not be put off with promises. When something was wrong, Zapata demanded that it be remedied immediately. He became so militant that Don Ignacio complained about him to the governor of Morelos, Pablo Escandon, a Diaz-appointed politician.

At the time, Morelos was suffering from a rash of bandit gangs that marauded from mountain hideouts.

Governor Escandon had an unusual way of dealing with the *bandidos*. Instead of executing those his Rurales captured, he had the outlaws conscripted into the army for a number of years. This removed them from Morelos and supplied troops for the army.

Although Zapata was no bandit, he was a troublemaker, according to Don Ignacio. And when Don Ignacio asked the governor to do something about Emiliano, it was promptly done. Zapata was arrested on a trumped-up charge, sent before a bribed magistrate, and sentenced to serve seven years in the army.

Emiliano did well as a soldier, rising to the rank of sergeant. He was discharged in September 1910, along with several thousand others, under the terms of a general amnesty granted by President Diaz to celebrate the national centenary.

Instead of groveling gratefully, Zapata returned to his village, recruited some friends, and formed his own outlaw band—but one that was different. The Zapatistas were not only out for loot; they raised political demands as well, demands such as the restoration of village lands confiscated by the hacendados years before.

"Tierra y Libertad!"—"Land and Liberty!"—was the Zapatista slogan. The peons heard and approved.

Writing of Zapata, a historian has said: "He was a man of no learning, of no broad social contacts, a simple, vigorous human being . . . but he knew that his people had been robbed of their lands and that it was his mission in life to return these lands to them."

Zapata sided with Madero when La Revolucion came and threw himself wholeheartedly into the cause. Between the years 1910 and 1919, amidst turmoil and violence, Zapata would provide the only viable government in Morelos and neighboring states.

9

EXIT DIAZ

In 1911, La Revolucion gained momentum. It spread because the Diaz regime was rotten with corruption. Although, on the surface, the dictatorship seemed solid enough, rot and decay lay just beneath the veneer. Had Diaz governed a sound regime, Madero's rebellion would have been crushed, although El Presidente could no longer have refused to make social reforms. At the first shock of the insurrection, the weaknesses of the administration were exposed. Right off it was apparent that the army, the bulwark of any dictatorship, lacked the means to deal with the uprising. During the years of the dictatorship, it had grown fat, flabby, and corrupt.

According to the muster rolls, the standing army numbered thirty thousand officers and men. In reality, it contained less than eighteen thousand. The officers, strutting about in polished boots, clanking spurs, fancy uniforms, and gold braid, were dishonest almost to the man. They stole from company mess funds, from payrolls, from the quartermaster—wherever a peso could be pilfered. Sergeants and corporals took what the officers left.

Rank and file soldiers were poor fighting material. Army service was a punishment passed by judges for minor offenses, and often for nothing at all. Men thrown into the army rather than jail made reluctant soldiers at best.

Poorly clothed, badly trained, ineptly led, paid only a pittance, the Mexican army was no first-rate fighting force. Thousands of conscripts awaited a chance to desert. Few had any wish to fight rebellious peons and recalcitrant workers, men like themselves—exploited and poverty-stricken.

But there were still quite a few soldiers who enjoyed shooting people; some actually believed in Diaz and were ready to fight out of principle. As a rule, the officers were loyal to the dictator, and Diaz could always rely on the Rurales when rebels had to be liquidated.

Neither Diaz nor his associates seemed concerned about Madero's Revolution. They chose to regard it as of no consequence and felt sure it would be over quickly. "This uprising is unimportant," Don Porfirio stated. "I promise that if the rebels ever reach five thousand in number, I shall take the field myself, despite my years."

Francisco Madero gave himself less chance for success than did Diaz. He made no move to take the offensive and waited in Texas for something favorable to happen.

The longer Madero lingered on United States soil, the more Diaz protested to Washington, stressing that it was against international law to permit a revolutionary group to mount an expedition against a friendly power.

According to Diaz, Madero was running his rebellion from the sanctuary of Texas. However, this time United States officials took no action against Madero. Washington was getting even for Diaz's refusal to let the U.S. Navy have its base at Magdalena Bay.

But after about four months, Washington had to order Madero out of Texas. Federal marshals armed with a warrant for his arrest arrived in San Antonio. Warned in advance, Madero fled and crossed the Rio Grande again on February 14, 1911. This time a force of about five hundred peasants met him with cheers and flowers.

In Mexico once more, Madero decided to attack. On March 6, he assaulted the border town of Casas Grandes. The rebels fought poorly and were badly organized; but the defending troops performed even worse. A white flag of surrender was raised from the town hall.

Then, just as the jubilant rebels were surging toward Casas Grandes, a federal relief column appeared and Madero's victorious soldiers broke and ran. Madero was hit in the wrist by a stray bullet. He counted casualties of fifty-one killed, about the same number wounded, and more than twenty captured. Madero also suffered the loss of guns, ammunition, and his only artillery piece. The revolt in Chihuahua, in all northern Mexico, seemed to have reached a disastrous end.

But luck was with Madero.

On March 7, the day after the Casas Grandes affair, President of the United States William Howard Taft ordered twenty thousand troops to the Mexican border for "maneuvers." Actually, Taft believed Diaz would not be able to control the situation much longer. If so, large American holdings in Mexico might be endangered. To further insure American interests, the U.S. Navy prepared to hold exercises off the west coast of Mexico. When it came to investments, Taft believed in preparedness.

Diaz misread Taft's reasons for all that military movement. He thought the United States meant to intervene on Madero's behalf. The old fox decided to end things while he was still ahead. Jose Limantour, his right-hand man, was out of the country on government business. Diaz asked him to try some behind-the-scenes negotiations on neutral ground.

Meetings between Limantour and representatives of Madero were held in an expensive suite on the fourth floor of New York City's luxurious Hotel Astor. (Diaz footed the bill.) Limantour proved quite pliable and surprised the Maderistas by agreeing to meet most of their demands—if Diaz approved. But despite the cordial atmosphere and congenial talk, nothing concrete came of the Hotel Astor discussions.

While Limantour and the Maderistas were dealing in

New York, fresh fighting broke out along the border. The rebels regrouped and struck at several towns to make up for the rout at Casas Grandes. The most successful of these forays took place around the border town of Agua Prieta.

That battle was witnessed by thousands of Americans who flocked to Douglas, Arizona, which was separated from Agua Prieta by the width of a street. The spectators ducked bullets, bet on the battle's outcome, and guzzled whiskey as fighting swirled on the opposite side of the street.

Madero's men finally chalked up their first victory by capturing Agua Prieta. The outcome of that battle caused some consternation in Mexico City. Diaz summoned foreign newsmen to the National Palace for a press conference. He said: "There have been slight disturbances of public order. They are of no importance. The government, with the means at its disposal, expects to reestablish complete order in a short time."

The reporters dutifully took down his words—which they had heard before—but the comment of an American reporter revealed the thinking in journalistic circles. He said, "I'll bet a month's pay Diaz is scared stiff. He can't put down this rebellion any more than I can walk across the Gulf of Mexico."

El Presidente must have realized that there were meager means at his disposal to subdue Madero. The dry rot in the army became more obvious daily. Troops called for active duty lacked supplies ranging from shoes to guns.

Despite the shortages, Diaz ordered large numbers of reinforcements rushed to the north, where reports indicated that the Maderistas had far more than five thousand men in action. The aged dictator apparently had forgotten his pledge to take the field if the enemy grew that strong.

Instead of leading his troops in battle, Diaz fumbled

about in his office poring over outdated maps, sending confused orders to his generals, ranting at cowed aides, and demanding that the press play up even the slightest clash with the rebels as a tremendous government victory.

In obedience to Diaz's command, trainloads of sad-faced soldiers rolled out of Mexico City for the northern border regions. But en route large numbers deserted. The men cast away their rifles, dumped their packs, ripped insignias off uniforms, and vanished into the rugged countryside.

Desertions were widespread and commonplace. In one cavalry regiment, eighty men were sent to water horses outside Ciudad Juarez. Neither they nor the horses ever were seen again.

Surprisingly, many hundreds of soldiers remained loyal to Diaz and moved up to the fighting front. But even these faithful warriors became disillusioned. Unit after unit discovered in combat that much of their ammunition was faulty; it had been purchased cheaply by General Manuel Mondragon, the army's commander. He had pocketed the difference between the regular price and what he had paid for the worthless cartridges.

When this shameful condition was exposed, the army's morale, never very good, sank to a new low. The rate of desertion leaped upward and climbed steadily higher despite summary executions ordered by drumhead courts-martial. For the first time in all the years of the Diaz regime, doubt and gloom assailed the dictator and his cronies.

On his return from New York, Limantour urged Diaz to announce sweeping reforms and concessions. Swallowing pride and vanity, El Presidente heeded him. Diaz went before Congress on April 1, 1911, and delivered a remarkably uncharacteristic speech. He declared that he was opposed to reelection—an amazing statement from a man in his eighth term as president. Diaz also claimed that all the demands, reforms, and concessions put forth by Madero had long been on his government's agenda and would gradually be implemented.

Like a sinner at confession, Diaz admitted he had committed excesses, that his administration had neglected the needs of the people and denied them rights; all this soon would change, he promised. There was no need to prolong a civil war, pitting brother against brother.

If Diaz believed his speech would persuade Madero to call off La Revolucion, he must have been sorely disappointed. Diaz's willingness to grant reforms only served to spur on the revolutionaries because they sensed that the old man was weakening. They felt victory was near.

Madero replied promptly and bluntly. In the name of the Revolution, he called on Diaz to resign immediately. Only this and nothing else could induce the Maderistas to stop fighting.

Actually, Madero could well afford to be stern. His forces were making new gains daily. Most of northern Mexico had been wrested from the control of Diaz. But Madero was not completely satisfied. He did not like some of the men who had come belatedly to his side. Many were local politicians who had entered his camp only because of personal ambition; with Diaz fading, these unscrupulous and unprincipled men wanted to be with the winner. However, they professed acceptance of the Plan of San Luis Potosi, and Madero had to take allies where he could find them.

As the anti-Diaz movement gathered strength, there were signs in early April that the tide of subversion had reached the capital. Pro-Maderistas grew bolder. Posters demanding the ouster of El Presidente were tacked up on walls, fences, and telegraph poles. Crowds swarmed through slum streets shouting support for Madero. Neither police, soldiers, nor bravistas interfered with the demonstrators. Newspapers denouncing the government were not shut down or their editors punished. The tide was shifting from Diaz to Madero.

Vice-President Ramon Corral did not care to await the final outcome. On April 12, he left Mexico for Paris, taking with him a fortune in cash that he had embezzled over the years. When he heard about Corral, Diaz tartly said, "The rat has left the sinking ship, eh? Well, we're still afloat. And when I get out of this mess, I shall deal with Corral in the manner he deserves."

Although few unprejudiced observers held out much hope for a Diaz military victory, the generals who owed career and fortune to El Presidente still waged desperate war in the north.

The struggle became sharper and uglier. Neither side gave or asked for quarter; both were equally guilty of atrocities. All captured rebels were shot; all federal officers taken prisoner were killed. Privates, corporals, and sergeants received the choice of joining the rebels or facing a firing squad; naturally, most accepted the former alternative.

Wild outlaw bands raised the banner of La Revolucion and committed many needless depredations. They wantonly destroyed property, burned churches, blew up schools, slaughtered livestock, and robbed trains. For some criminal types, the Revolution offered a good opportunity to loot, rape, burn, plunder, and kill.

In spite of the crimes, brutality, and atrocities, the Mexican civil war still retained moments of a comic opera plot. American border towns such as El Paso and Douglas afforded a grandstand view of the war as fighting raged along the frontier.

Matrons of Douglas invited guests to what became known as "battle teas." When a skirmish broke out within view, the ladies gathered on the flat rooftops of houses that overlooked the battle area. Tea and cakes were served while the women watched the war through field glasses.

Occasionally, stray bullets found a mark among spectators. Several females were slain or wounded at battle teas. But the practice did not stop because of the danger. "It added to the excitement. There was that extra touch to make things even more thrilling," a Douglas housewife recalled.

Most Americans who lived on the border were sympathetic to Madero and helped him in numerous ways. Some El Paso residents smuggled guns to the Maderistas, and even a small brass cannon that played a decisive part in the capture of Ciudad Juarez.

A number of foreigners felt strongly enough to join up and fight for Madero. One such man was an American, Dr. Ira Bush, who became chief surgeon of the revolutionary army. Adventurers and soldiers-of-fortune enlisted in the rebel cause, literally forming a sort of foreign legion. Among these were Giuseppe Garibaldi, the Italian liberator's grandson; Ben Viljoen, formerly a Boer general; A. W. Lewis, a Canadian machine gunner, a free-lance soldier who roved the world seeking out wars; a dapper Frenchman named Louis Carpentier, who was a virtuoso of artillery.

The Americans fighting for Madero were an oddly assorted crew. Best known of these gringos were Sam Dreben, nicknamed "the Fighting Jew" because he had been in half a dozen wars, mainly Central American revolutions, and Oscar Creighton, a New York stockbroker grown tired of Wall Street; Creighton won renown as "the Dynamite Kid" because of his skill with the explosive. Also on Madero's side was an El Paso cowboy named Tom Mix, later to win fame and fortune as a Hollywood western movie star.

As the fighting in the north continued, the rebels captured town after town. The federals were pushed back toward Mexico City, but not even the capital offered much of a sanctuary. Emiliano Zapata and his peons were overrunning Morelos and closing in on Mexico City. The pincers of history were clamping on Diaz as state capitals all over Mexico began falling to the Maderistas.

Suffering terribly from an infected jaw, Diaz agreed to a peace treaty with the Maderistas. It was signed at Ciudad Juarez on May 21, 1911. In the pact, Diaz agreed to resign and Francisco de la Barra was to become provisional president pending an election in which no one doubted that Madero would be the overwhelming choice. When news of the treaty was publicly released, spontaneous demonstrations broke out in Mexico City as jubilant people danced in the streets.

Although he had agreed to resign, Diaz refused to surrender his office. When the demonstrators learned of this, a huge throng formed outside Diaz's home in the Calle Cadena and shouted for his ouster.

During the next several days, the street crowds grew larger and larger. On May 24, a tremendous mass congregated in the Zocalo before the National Palace. Eyewitnesses estimated that upwards of seventy-five thousand persons were jammed into the plaza. Eight months earlier these same people had cheered Diaz in that very place. Now they were there to demand that he quit.

The dictator clung tenaciously to his office. Flushed with fever, his face twisted in pain, he stubbornly spurned the advice of aides who counseled him to resign before it was too late. The roaring mobs outside sounded menacing as their prior good humor dissolved into sullen rancor. Soon restiveness would become violence.

That night the sky darkened with rain clouds; distant lightning flashed, far-off thunder rumbled, and blood was spilled in the Zocalo. The army and the police were well prepared for trouble. A dozen Maxim machine guns had been emplaced on the roof of the National Palace. Platoons of riflemen crouched in the towers of the cathedral to the north. On the south side of the Zocalo, more soldiers and machine gunners had been strategically posted.

At about 9:00 P.M., mounted police sallied out of the

65

palace courtyard to clear the grounds of demonstrators. They made three attempts, but each time the defiant mob beat them back.

Half an hour later, the police charged again, firing revolvers over the heads of the people. This infuriated the demonstrators, who rushed the horsemen. A riot broke out. Police swung sabers, clubs, and carbines. Shots were fired. Wounded and bleeding rioters stumbled away from the melee or lay sprawled on the cobblestones.

The police probably could have handled the disorder without any help, but a panicky army lieutenant thought the mob had gotten out of control. He ordered riflemen on the cathedral tower to open fire. Volleys poured down into the crowd. Men fell dead, women shrieked, bawling children were knocked down and trampled to death as bullets splattered into the milling, frantic mass.

When the riflemen started shooting, the machine gunners on the National Palace roof also let loose a barrage. The Maxims chattered as gunners ran through belt after belt of cartridges. Streams of lead slashed down for nearly five minutes. Scores were killed. The frenzied mob clawed and fought to escape the Zocalo, which had become a deathtrap.

Suddenly, a flash of lightning split the black sky and a shattering thunderclap heralded a cloudburst. Rain beat down on Mexico City in solid sheets. Drenched and frightened, the demonstrators crept home leaving dead and wounded behind. The pelting rain washed the blood from the cobblestones.

Police and army officials tried to make the shooting in the Zocalo seem like a minor skirmish. Official reports listed only seven dead and forty wounded. But at one police station alone, a foreign reporter counted more than 150 bodies awaiting identification. Doctors in Mexico City hospitals admitted to having treated over one thousand gunshot wounds.

The tragic occurrence in the Zocalo finally made Diaz

see that he must resign. Late in the afternoon of May 25, Diaz penned his own resignation, his final word to the Mexican people.

His statement was read out to an emergency session of Congress. The legislators greeted it in silence; but when the men whom Diaz had called "my tame horses" voted to accept his ouster, the packed public galleries rocked with cheering and applause.

Parades formed in the streets. All at once, bands appeared and happy music echoed in the capital. Everyone joined the celebration—peons, police, factory workers, housewives, beggars, students, soldiers. It was a joyful, spontaneous outburst by a people too long repressed.

As the revelry reached its height, men still loyal to Diaz planned to get him safely out of the country. That night, El Presidente, his wife, son, daughter-in-law, and five grandchildren sneaked out of the house on Calle Cadena, leaving behind all their furniture and possessions, taking with them only the clothes they wore.

Three special trains waited to speed the party to Veracruz. Three hundred picked troops under General Victoriano Huerta rode the first and third trains. The cars of the middle one carried Diaz and his family. As the engines chuffed out of Colonia Railroad Station and rolled onto the Veracruz tracks, Diaz wryly remarked, "I came to Mexico City in a hail of bullets and perhaps I shall have to leave in the same way."

He proved to be an accurate prophet. Rebels attacked the trains, but were driven off by Huerta's soldiers after a sharp fight.

Diaz reached Veracruz and took refuge in the home of a British businessman for nearly a week while awaiting a ship to Europe. At last, on May 31, weeping bitterly, Diaz and his entourage boarded the German steamer *Ypiranga* and sailed off into exile.

Diaz reached Paris in June. There he lived modestly and economically, in sharp contrast to other Mexican exiles of his regime. Limantour, who reached Paris a week after Diaz, dwelled luxuriously on money he had embezzled from the national treasury. Most exiles had lined their pockets out of public funds, but Diaz had never enriched himself in office. He lived simply in a run-down flat until July 2, 1915, when he died.

The man who toppled Diaz made ready to accept the fruits of his victory. On June 3, Madero started for Mexico City by rail from his home in Parras, Coahuila, seven hundred miles away.

The train moved slowly through the rugged country, stopping at bridges, stations, crossings, and water towers to be greeted by many thousands of men, women, and children gathered along the right-of-way.

The people cheered him with fervor. Women held up babies to be kissed by him. The sick, lame, and blind begged Madero to touch them, for they regarded him, quite mistakenly, as a savior or a saint and believed he had God-given powers to cure by the laying on of hands. At almost every stop Madero delivered a speech, and the journey from Parras to Mexico City stretched out for four days.

More than 250,000 people came to the capital for a glimpse of the new national hero. Thousands slept in parks, doorways, or on the streets. The morning of June 7, while the overcrowded capital slumbered, Mexico City was shaken by the severest earthquake in the city's living memory. The shock lasted fourteen minutes and was recorded in places as far off as Sydney, Australia; Portland, Oregon; Bombay, India; and London, England.

Yawning fissures appeared in sidewalks and roadways. Sleeping men, women, and children were hurled from their beds and buried beneath tons of debris as buildings collapsed. Great sparks snapped from severed electrical cables; blue flames danced high as gas mains broke; bursting water pipes sent geysers high into the air.

An ancient church crumbled in ruins. The city's main

barracks caved in, killing many soldiers. A wide crack split a wall of the National Palace. The railroad depot was demolished. Shards of glass rained down on the streets in crystal showers.

Screaming thousands dashed from swaying houses to fall on their knees in frenetic prayer. The superstitious said that this was Satan's punishment for the deposing of his son, Porfirio Diaz.

When the quake finally died away, panic gripped the city. Many who had escaped unscathed through the awful fourteen minutes of the shock were knocked down and trampled by hysterical mobs.

This devastation was indeed an inauspicious entry to Mexico City for Madero. But, within hours, the people seemed to have forgotten the catastrophe. When Madero alighted from his train later that day, smiling crowds greeted him. People swarmed around laughing, crying, shouting, struggling to reach him, to kiss his hands, to embrace him.

A cavalry troop managed to clear a path for the frail man who had defeated the dictator. It took more than four hours for Madero to traverse the two miles from the wreckage of the railroad station through the rubble-littered streets to reach the National Palace.

There, one of the first revolutionary leaders to give him the traditional *abrazo*—hug—was Emiliano Zapata, who had made one of his infrequent trips to the capital from Morelos. Zapata wanted to be on the spot when the new leader of Mexico arrived.

Madero was so exhausted by the excitement of his trip and tumultuous welcome that he went to a house that his parents owned and slept for a full twenty-four hours. He did not then know that these would probably comprise the last restful hours he was to pass in Mexico City.

PART

II

The Idealist

10

"HE HAS UNLEASHED A TIGER!"

Francisco Madero possessed several qualities needed by a successful revolutionary—idealism, dedication, and courage. But he lacked the most essential trait—ruthlessness. Madero was obsessed by the need always to do the right thing. A well-intentioned but inept politician, he sought fair play in a game where the only rule was survival.

After having pushed out Diaz, Madero seemed to feel that everything else would fall automatically into place. Somewhat overwhelmed by the reception the people had given him, dazzled by the adulation showered upon him, Madero failed to realize that though Diaz was gone, many of his closest collaborators remained. Hundreds, perhaps thousands, of men who had been befriended by the old dictator still held influential posts in government, army, church, business, and banking circles.

A ruthless revolutionary would have eliminated these survivors of the former regime and surrounded himself with his own picked men. But Madero shrank from what he regarded as unnecessary bloodshed. He had forgotten, or else never had known, the revolutionary adage "You can't make an omelet without breaking eggs." In short, bloodshed and revolution were soulmates. One went with the other.

Madero's need to treat everyone with fairness made him vulnerable to the surviving Diazistas. Instead of calling for an immediate election, Madero chose to wait until

October 1. In the meantime, the reins of government were held by the provisional president, Francisco de la Barra; Madero had given up his claim to that post in favor of de la Barra.

This was a grave error. De la Barra was one hundred percent a Diaz man. Madero's endorsement of him checked the progress of the Revolution. De la Barra was not the man to implement the reforms in the Plan of San Luis Potosi. A well-educated professional diplomat, he had represented Mexico in several foreign countries. At the outbreak of the Madero Revolution, de la Barra had been the Mexican ambassador to the United States.

His polished manner masked the fact that he was little more than a Diaz lackey and could not have gone far without the help of the old dictator. Someone once described de la Barra as a "marshmallow made up to look like a man." Clearly, he should not have been in the saddle with Mexico rearing like an untamed bronco. The country required a strong hand and a sharp mind to guide it through the troubled time ahead. The country needed Madero—or at least the kind of leader the people fancied Madero to be.

A more astute man than Madero would easily have seen that de la Barra was not the person for the job. The provisional president was an equivocator. He told his first cabinet meeting: "I did not seek nor do I want to be president of Mexico even for a short time. The happiest day of my life will be that on which I shall relinquish this onerous task."

However, there was no exit for de la Barra at the moment. For the next five months, at least, he was slated to be the president of the Republic. De la Barra had at least one point in his favor. Neither the Diazistas nor the Maderistas had anything bad to hold against him. He took no strong stands on any issues, and both sides regarded him as harmless. As one observer said, "De la Barra might not have been much of a president, but he certainly proved to be one hell of a tightrope walker."

Thus, with a nonentity at its head, the Revolution took over Mexico. Since there had been much disruption and upheaval in government circles, a great many posts, ranging from state governorships to postal clerks, were unfilled. A scramble for these jobs began as Diazistas and Maderistas vied for the positions and promotions to be dispensed by de la Barra. Madero stood off to one side, behaving as if he were above such mundane matters as doling out jobs. At this point, Madero's only contribution seemed to be lofty talk of uniting the disparate groups in Mexico by means of honest dealings and fair play.

His beaming goodwill did little to settle down the country. Some of his people were growing disgruntled at the way things were working out. However, Pancho Villa was perfectly satisfied. The fearsome bandit-rebel, pleased at having helped Madero to victory, hung up his gun belt, returned to Chihuahua city, married a longtime sweetheart, Luz Corral, and opened a wholesale meat business.

But other revolutionary generals, having had a taste of power during the fighting, were reluctant to give it up. Going back to civilian ways, tilling the soil or working in a factory, no longer held any appeal. These men believed they had earned the right to commissions in the regular army. Others thought Madero should reward them with important government posts.

For some imponderable reason Madero chose to ignore the men who had fought and won the Revolution for him. When one of his former generals, Pascual Orozco, asked Madero's help in obtaining a regular army commission, Madero shunted him aside. Instead, he was made military commandant in Chihuahua state without receiving the rank to go with the post or a commission in the regulars.

Even less comprehensible than his cavalier treatment of Orozco was Madero's willingness to comply when the interim government ordered all rebel troops disbanded and paid off. Rebel leaders bitterly complained that the Revolution was being betrayed. With revolutionary forces demobilized, the only armed troops in the country would be the regular army, which had fought against the rebels. It simply did not make much sense to turn Mexico back to the foes of La Revolucion. But once more Madero gave his followers the cold shoulder.

The disbanding of the rebel armies did not go off smoothly. In Morelos, Emiliano Zapata defied de la Barra's order and refused to demobilize his tough partisans until the promised land reforms were carried out. Madero went to Cuernavaca at de la Barra's request. That town, only forty-seven miles from Mexico City, was in the dead center of Zapatista country.

Zapata apparently was impressed by Madero's sincerity and agreed to a partial disbandment of his fighters on condition that every man be given some land of his own. Madero not only agreed to this, but also promised each one a payment of a hundred pesos for handing over his rifle and ammunition. More than seven hundred Zapatistas quickly accepted the offer.

Madero returned to Mexico City and happily announced that Zapata no longer presented a problem. It seemed as though this were quite true. By the end of July many Zapatistas had turned in their weapons. But the clouds began gathering again when the government failed to give the discharged rebels parcels of land.

Zapata demanded a meeting with de la Barra, but the provisional president refused to deal with him. Haughtily he remarked, "I find it truly disagreeable that an individual with antecedents such as Zapata's should be permitted an interview with the president of the Republic."

This statement naturally angered Zapata. He was further provoked when de la Barra sent troops under General Victoriano Huerta into Cuernavaca. The general, a longtime Diaz supporter, had commanded the escort when the dictator fled to Veracruz. Huerta detested Zapata and was bitterly hated in return. The general's orders were to disarm Zapata's people "by any means deemed necessary." When he heard this, Zapata stopped demobilizing and warned his men to make ready for a fight.

During that month of July 1911, the victorious Revolution seemed to be unraveling like an old torn sweater. In many areas federal troops and former rebels clashed. The revolutionaries were growing increasingly suspicious of the government. To their dismay, they discovered that the old gang still called the tune. The cientificos and others of the Diaz clique ran the army, state and national legislatures, and municipal governments. The Rurales still rode roughshod. The haciendas remained intact. The landless still had no land. The workers still toiled at starvation wages. All was as if the Revolution had never taken place.

Had La Revolucion, that object of so many dreams and hopes, actually been betrayed? It appeared that way to men who had risked their lives and shed blood to bring change to Mexico. It was even more upsetting to them that Francisco Madero, the saint of the Revolution, appeared to be more anxious to win favor with the provisional government than to fulfill the promises he had made to the people.

The bitter and disillusioned masses began to suspect that Madero had sold them out. Anger seized men whose visions of freedom were dissolving. Once, they had turned their wrath on Diaz. Now Madero was the target. Grievous trouble was brewing unless Madero went back to the way of La Revolucion. Men who had nothing to lose but their lives would not shrink from risking them again and again until dreams became reality.

Just before he embarked on the *Ypiranga*, Diaz had said to an aide, "I feel sorry for Madero. He has unleashed a tiger. Let us see if he can control the beast."

The tiger was loose now and snarling.

11

"THE WILD-LOOKING BANDS
RODE IN . . ."

The summer of 1911 was hot with long, dusty dry
spells followed by days of heavy tropical rains. But the
bad weather was only a minor annoyance in troubled
Mexico.

The center of discontent was the state of Morelos,
where Zapata continued to demand that the government
keep its pledge of land to the peons. Late in August,
Madero made another trip to Cuernavaca and conferred
with Zapata, who agreed to demobilize when Huerta and
his troops were withdrawn.

This seemed reasonable enough to Madero, who then
asked de la Barra to comply with the request. Instead,
de la Barra sent reinforcements to Huerta and reiterated
his orders that the Zapatistas be disarmed.

The outcome of this action was predictable. Zapatistas and federal troops clashed near Chinameca on
August 30. That skirmish marked the opening of a fresh
rebellion in Morelos. Fighting continued through September, even as Zapata called upon the government to
negotiate a peaceable settlement. But de la Barra was
adamant. Before any talks could take place the Zapatistas
must lay down their arms and surrender to Huerta.
Zapata rejected this and the shooting continued.

Through some quirk of illogic, Madero refused to

place the responsibility for the Morelos uprising where it belonged. Instead of branding de la Barra with the blame, Madero insisted that Huerta was guilty and repeatedly called for his removal.

A bald, bullet-headed man, General Victoriano Huerta suffered from weak eyes, a condition remedied by thick-lensed steel-framed glasses. He also had an insatiable yen for cognac and drank incredible quantities of it every day.

However, Huerta's drinking did not interfere with his military abilities. A top-notch soldier, he earned grudging respect even from Zapata by the way he handled his troops in the field.

Huerta ran a tough campaign. He pushed his men, pressed the Zapatistas, and guzzled cognac by the bottle. One observer noted, "Although Huerta drank so much every night that he had to be led to his bed, he was up early the next morning, looking as though he were not so much as acquainted with the smell of cognac."

General Huerta was vigorously prosecuting his anti-Zapata drive with some success when Madero's complaints about him finally bore fruit. Huerta was relieved as commander of federal forces in Morelos at the end of September. The alcoholic general vowed to have revenge on Madero. So vehement was he that an observer later recalled, "I marveled at the remarkable innocence of Madero, who seemed to think he could play fast and loose with a man like Huerta."

At the moment, Madero had deeper problems to face than Huerta's anger. With presidential elections due on October 1, Madero had caused a split among his followers by choosing for vice-president an obscure journalist named Jose Pino Suarez over the favorite of the Maderistas, Dr. Vasquez Gomez.

It made no sense for Madero to pick Pino Suarez. Vasquez Gomez had been with him since the San Antonio days, while Pino Suarez had not even participated in the

Revolution. This unexplained behavior by Madero alienated Vasquez Gomez's many friends. But when election day rolled around, the Mexican people showed they still had faith in Madero despite his blunders. He received more than 90 percent of the popular vote. His chief opponent was General Bernardo Reyes, who had never given up on the presidency.

The voters were in no mood for General Reyes, and wherever he appeared hostile crowds hooted him down. After the election, Reyes crossed over the Rio Grande to San Antonio and busied himself with gathering followers for an uprising against Madero.

On November 6, 1911, Madero was inaugurated president of Mexico. His administration was off to a bad start right at the inaugural ceremonies. Complete confusion held sway. Spectators pushed and shoved and got into fistfights. Important foreign dignitaries were barred from the chambers where the swearing in took place. A newspaperman noted that the inauguration was as chaotic as the state of the nation.

As he took the oath of office, Madero seemed blissfully unaware that he was surrounded by strong and influential enemies. First were the former Diazistas—the cientificos, regular army officers, landowners, and church hierarchy. Though their leader was gone, these men still hoped to take power. Indeed, many of them still held important government posts.

Businessmen made up the second anti-Madero group. Mexicans, Americans, Europeans, Orientals—they stood implacably opposed to Madero and all he represented. From the very beginning, the business interests had been aligned against Madero and had done everything possible to defeat the Revolution. Now that it was victorious, they plotted to sabotage the new regime and bring it to an untimely end.

Madero should have been alert to the dangers from these factions, but he never dreamed that his administra-

tion also would be imperiled from within the revolution-
ary movement itself. Every day, discontent and dissension
increased among the rebels. Zapata was already in revolt.
Others, like Pascual Orozco, were embittered because the
Revolution had not satisfied their personal ambitions;
Orozco therefore was turning against Madero.

The president decided that he must settle the Zapata
rebellion at once. Immediately after his inauguration,
Madero sent negotiators to Zapata with an offer of freedom and no reprisals if he would surrender uncondition-
ally. But by then it was too late for compromise: Zapata,
who had been nicknamed "the Attila of the South," was in
no mood for conciliation. Too much blood had been spilled,
too many false promises made, for Zapata to trust the
new government any more than he had trusted the old.

Zapata had remained the most idealistic of the leading figures of the Revolution. He fought single-mindedly
to regain the peon's land and to raise his status economically, politically, and socially. Zapata probably knew
little of communism or Karl Marx; he was a communist
by instinct rather than indoctrination, a revolutionary
missionary who cried out for "Land and Liberty!"

He had only one cause, the struggle to better the
lives of the poor; he had but one enemy, the social system
that permitted poverty and its allied ills—ignorance,
disease, misery, and early death. Zapata rallied to his side
the wretched, the landless, the hungry. They responded
to his ringing cry: *"Men of the south! It is better to die
on your feet than to live on your knees!"*

He had risen in rebellion when the Plan of San Luis
Potosi was initially proclaimed. His followers were clad
in rags, a barefoot, weaponless horde. But in a short time
he was able to boast: "We have begged from outside not
one bullet, not one rifle, not one peso. Everything we
have, we have taken from the enemy."

To Madero's emissaries Zapata repeated his oft
stated demand: land for the masses. When that was

granted and only then would he consider putting down his gun. But Madero had given no land and would not now give it on a wholesale scale.

So Zapata carried on with his revolt and on November 28, 1911, standing on a table in a mountain hut, he announced the program of his rebellion. Zapata called it the Plan of Ayala after a famous hacienda located nearby. Before he read out his Plan, a Mexican flag was raised to the tune of a band playing the national anthem.

Zapata had drawn up a truly revolutionary program. Among other things, he called for: the seizure of all foreign-owned land and all properties taken from the villagers in the past; the confiscation of one-third of the land held by hacendados friendly to the Revolution and full confiscation against owners directly or indirectly opposed to the Plan of Ayala.

Further, Zapata demanded the extradition, arrest, trial, and execution of Diaz, Corral, Limantour, and others; the expulsion from Mexico of all Spaniards; the absorption of all revolutionary forces into one national army "to prevent aggression by foreign powers." Surprisingly, Zapata also declared full support of the Plan of San Luis Potosi. Apparently his breach with Madero was not irreparable.

Anyone who doubted that Zapata intended to implement the Plan of Ayala was quickly disenchanted. All land captured by Zapatistas was immediately turned over to the peons. Soon, peasant huts and shacks dotted the arable fields on some of the country's richest haciendas. The land, Zapata stated, had been seized and distributed "in the sovereign cause of liberty and equality." It was proof that Zapata's slogan of "Land and Liberty!" was not an empty one and it brought thousands of peons flocking to his banner—a black flag emblazoned with a death's head.

The Zapatistas moved across Morelos in a human tide, and before long Cuernavaca fell to them without a battle.

A witness described the entry of Zapata's people into the town:

> They were a wild-looking body of men, undisciplined, half-clothed, mounted on half-starved horses. Grotesque and obsolete weapons . . . were clasped in their hands, thrust through their belts, or slung across their saddles. . . . But they rode in as heroes and conquerors and the pretty Indian girls met them with kisses and flowers. . . . All afternoon the wild-looking bands rode in . . . I shall remember them always.

Even as he launched this rebellion under the Plan of Ayala, Zapata was willing to compromise. He had hoped for the governorship of Morelos state—a sign that Madero believed in and trusted him. Madero was still able to win the goodwill of the so-called "Attila of the South," but instead committed another of his inconceivable blunders.

The governorship of Morelos went, not to Zapata, but to a general named Ambrosio Figuero, who owned a large estate in Morelos. This appointment incensed the Zapatistas and convinced them that nothing could be expected from Madero. As a result, the revolt dragged on, a constant source of embarrassment to Madero and a drain on the shaky finances of the government.

Troubles even more acute than the Zapata uprising shook the Madero administration. The president had held out to the people shiny promises that he thought to fulfill over a period of time. But once again Madero had erred. He had misjudged the temper of the Mexican people. They no longer had the patience to wait for a better existence. They wanted the improvements to start at once. They demanded an immediate break with the awful past. They were calling for miracles; unfortunately, Madero was no miracle worker.

He was a man who acted with painstaking caution after mulling over every detail of a problem. To him, each reform presented an intellectual exercise that had to be discussed and dissected—but not acted upon. He did not seem to realize that emergency conditions existed in Mexico. Overwhelmed by revolutionary ardor, Madero had promised land to the landless. But, once in power, he did nothing about cutting up the huge estates and handing them over to the people.

When the masses saw that Madero's words were only words and not deeds, they acted on their own. Poor peasants swarmed out and took land for themselves. Squatters came like locusts and held the land. Madero was shocked by this illegal procedure. He called upon the squatters to clear out, and when they refused he did not hesitate to send troops who drove them off the land at bayonet point. Once this happened, the peons, who had risked their lives for Madero in battle, turned on him.

Every compromise he offered was rejected by the land-hungry peasants. Madero's pleas for patience were hooted down. "We have been patient long enough! Patience is a luxury we no longer can afford!" a peasant leader cried.

Surrounded by growing discontent on every side, ringed in by duplicity and hypocrisy, Madero was a baffled, bewildered man. "I have wanted only the best for the people. Why do they now seek to destroy me?" he lamented.

Every day the government floundered a bit more. Madero seemed incapable of coping with the flood of complex problems besetting him. As he wrestled with ever increasing difficulties, not the least of which was Zapata's revolt, a second rebellion, this one led by that old war-horse, General Bernardo Reyes, burst upon him.

- 12 -

"I'M NOT A DAMNED
BOOKKEEPER!"

Luckily for Madero, the Reyes rebellion ran its course more like slapstick comedy than a serious insurrection. General Reyes had nurtured his revolt in San Antonio from the same hotel that had served as Madero's headquarters. So bumblingly did Reyes conspire and plot that his plans leaked out to the American authorities.

President Taft was sick and tired of Mexicans using United States territory as a springboard for their uprisings, and he ordered Reyes arrested at once. Federal marshals nabbed the general and locked him up in San Antonio Jail, from which he was released on bond while awaiting trial.

Instead of wasting time, Reyes jumped bail on December 4, 1911, crossed the Rio Grande, and gathered a force of about six hundred men. He had expected to be joined by many hundreds more, counting on a mass defection of army officers to his side. He also thought that Diazistas and other assorted enemies of Madero would rally to him. But, as the days passed, nobody came. His original six hundred was depleted by desertions and dwindled to only a remnant.

On Christmas Day, 1911, the Reyes rebellion was quashed. A brief skirmish between his ragtag army and government troops ended with the surrender of Reyes to a longtime foe, General Jacinto Trevino. The rebels dispersed—every man for himself—and this revolution was over.

"I called upon the army. I called upon the people—but nobody answered . . . so I resolved to discontinue the war. . . . Now I need time to think things over," an embittered Reyes said. He had plenty of time to think in a cell of the military prison at Santiago Tlaltelolco in Mexico City.

The Reyes threat to Madero was almost effortlessly suppressed, but more revolts followed and these gave real trouble. A group of dissidents led by Dr. Francisco Vasquez Gomez, Madero's running mate in 1910, launched an insurrection in Chihuahua state. "I raise the standard of revolt because Madero is not abiding by the Plan of San Luis Potosi," said Vasquez Gomez.

As Madero moved to put down Vasquez Gomez, President Taft, heeding Ambassador Henry Lane Wilson's assertion that the government in Mexico City was shaky, rushed 34,000 regulars to the border and ordered an additional 66,000 national guardsmen to duty along the Rio Grande.

Taft's explanation for this mobilization, in February 1912, was that the Madero government could not protect American lives, property, and business interests in Mexico. At least this was the information Ambassador Wilson had passed on to Washington.

Taft warned that if there were any border fighting in which bullets or shells landed on American soil, United State troops would "move forcefully to safeguard Americans in the area." Madero construed this as a threat of armed U.S. intervention. Shaken by that prospect, he ordered his garrison at Ciudad Juarez not to resist if attacked because of the danger of shots crossing into the United States. As a result, Ciudad Juarez fell to Vasquez Gomez without resistance.

In March, Madero's troubles multiplied when General Pascual Orozco also revolted in Chihuahua, taking with him some six thousand well-armed troops. A brash and arrogant man, Orozco sent a telegram to Madero vowing to hang the president from "the highest tree in the Zocalo."

There were no high-principled motives in Orozco's rebellion. Madero had simply not rewarded him well enough. Frustrated and angry, Orozco poured out his complaints about Madero to anyone who would listen. Among those who listened were several millionaire cattle barons of Chihuahua. They found in the frustrated Orozco the perfect dupe for foiling projected land reforms, and sparked unrest and insurrection in northern Mexico aimed at overthrowing Madero.

Although Madero had pushed through only limited land reforms and did not seem inclined to do more, he was regarded as a menace by the cattle barons. Even Madero's few timid steps toward agrarian democracy were unacceptable to them.

The hacendados had little reason to complain. They had come out of the Revolution with hardly any loss. Except for the insignificant acreage Madero had parceled out to a handful of peons, the cattle barons' lives had not changed perceptibly.

Of all those wealthy men, the richest was Don Luis Terrazas, an eighty-one-year-old hacendado. In addition to vast estates, he owned banks, factories, public utilities, mines, and mills. Don Luis refused to relinquish any part of his empire. The slightest hint of democracy was repugnant to Don Luis and his fellow cattlemen. Since Madero seemed intent on bringing democratic changes to Mexico, they decided to get rid of him.

Orozco was the man for Don Luis and the other millionaires. They courted, praised, and beguiled him with flattery. It did not take long to buy Orozco. He would do anything they asked; and when Don Luis called upon him to revolt against Madero, he did. Well financed by his sponsors, he had money, arms, and ammunition.

Before Madero could make any moves, Orozco had taken most of Chihuahua state. Hampered by the Zapata rebellion in Morelos, Madero found it difficult to raise a force capable of coping with Orozco.

Initially, the only significant resistance to Orozco came from Pancho Villa. Completely loyal to Madero, Villa detested Orozco. When the Chihuahua revolt broke out, Villa left his wholesale meat business, strapped on his guns, and recruited men to fight the *insurrectos.*

Among those who hurried to join Villa was Tom Fountain, an American soldier of fortune. This was Fountain's sixth or seventh war; a crack machine gunner, he had fought in Central American revolutions for years, and also with the Maderistas. In all that warfare, Fountain was not even scratched. But this time, his luck ran out.

During a battle around Parral, Fountain was captured by Orozco's men. Next morning his captors let him loose. As he walked off, a group of Orozco's officers gunned him down from behind. Orozco whitewashed the murder. The official explanation for the slaying was "shot while trying to escape." The erstwhile revolutionary, Pascual Orozco, had revived the Diaz tactic of *ley fuga.*

His troops were called *Colorados*—Reds—by Mexicans, and Red Flaggers by Americans, because of the red flag under which they fought. (In Mexico, the red flag meant that an enemy could expect no mercy.)

The Red Flaggers terrorized northern Mexico, leaving a trail of death and suffering where they rode. Orozco's top commander, General Ynes Salazar, was the man responsible for most of the atrocities. He inflicted them with such relish that a journalist noted: "One cannot help but believe that Salazar gets pleasure from inflicting pain and causing grief. . . . He is a sick and vicious man."

Because of the acts committed by the Colorados,

Porfirio Diaz, El Presidente of Mexico, poses for a formal portrait in military uniform bedecked with medals and decorations.

Francisco I. Madero, who led the successful revolt against Diaz, stands on the steps of a train during a brief stop while on way to Mexico City. The diminutive Madero was deposed and executed after a year in office.

Francisco I. Madero
Pachuca Mex.

President Huerta (center) and his cabinet. Left to right: Rodolfo Reyes (minister of justice); Esquival Obregon (minister of finance); Francisco de la Barra (minister of foreign affairs); General Manuel Mondragon (minister of war); Vera Estanol (minister of education); Garcia Gernados (minister of interior); and Robles Gil (minister of state).

General Victoriano Huerta overthrew Madero and held Mexico in a dictatorial grip during his short term as president of the Republic.

One-armed General Alvaro Obregon sits for the camera shortly before winning the Mexican presidential election of 1920. In 1928, he was assassinated by a religious fanatic.

Underwood & Underwood

Rear Admiral Frank F. Fletcher, commanding U.S. naval units at Veracruz, reviews troops and bluejackets during a ceremony. With Admiral Fletcher are Nelson O'Shaughnessy (civilian clothes), U.S. chargé d'affaires, and General Frederick Funston, U.S. Army.

Underwood & Underwood

White-bearded President Venustiano Carranza, who followed Huerta to the presidency, stands at mid-span on the International Bridge over the Rio Grande. With him are members of his staff and U.S. Army officers. Photo was taken after Carranza conferred with American authorities.

Mounted on fast ponies, Zapatistas mass for attack on a suburb of Mexico City during their leader's revolt against Huerta.

Too often, scenes such as this were witnessed during Mexican Revolution. These six men are awaiting a firing squad. Note the wall pockmarked by bullets of prior executions.

Armed with a variety of rifles, bandoliered Villistas flank their leader, Pancho Villa (center). These men were among the toughest fighters in Mexico.

A column of U.S. infantry snakes over the barren terrain of northern Mexico in a vain pursuit of Pancho Villa following his raid on Columbus, New Mexico, in 1916.

Pancho Villa (center) is seated beside Emiliano Zapata (holding large sombrero) in the National Palace, Mexico City, on January 2, 1915. The man on Villa's right is former bandit chieftain Tomas Urbina.

Villa vowed to take vengeance on them. He ordered that no Colorado prisoner should be spared. "Eye for eye. Tooth for tooth. Brutality for brutality," Villa swore.

The Madero government was not able to mount any sort of counteroffensive against Orozco until March 24. By this time the Red Flaggers had spread ruin and havoc. The peons and townspeople who had suffered from Orozco's depredations were angered because the government had given them no protection. But during the last week of March 1912, more than eight thousand federal troops under Jose Gonzalez Salas, the minister of war, assisted by Generals Trucy Aubert and Aureliano Blanquet, moved against Orozco.

Gonzalez Salas and the main part of the federal army sped north by rail, while Aubert and Blanquet moved along the flanks. Orozco met the federals some eight hundred miles north of Mexico City at a town called Rellano. The train-borne federals were blown out of their cars by explosives planted along the track. Gonzalez Salas, who survived the blast, beat a hasty retreat south aboard a train which had not been damaged. The rest of his army was dispersed by Orozco's troops. When Gonzalez Salas learned the outcome of the battle near Rellano, he shot himself.

The Mexico City newspapers lambasted Madero for the defeat, because he had permitted Gonzalez Salas, a man with little military experience, to command the force. One newspaper, *El Pais*, called for the reinstatement of General Victoriano Huerta, an officer "who knew how to win."

Madero refused to call upon Huerta. "I don't trust a man who drinks the way he does," the president said. But his cabinet members felt differently.

"If you don't trust Huerta, keep him under surveillance," a presidential aide argued. "And what if he drinks, as long as he brings us victory? Lincoln put Grant in command even though Grant liked the bottle. You have no choice, Senor Presidente. Huerta is the only good general we have at present."

At last Madero yielded and placed the prosecution of the anti-Orozco campaign in Huerta's hands. The general assured the president, for whom he had neither liking nor respect, "I will whip him! This I guarantee! I will beat him!"

With Huerta in charge, matters looked up for the Maderistas. The alcoholic general snapped his troops into fighting shape. He was joined by Villa near Torreon. On May 10, Huerta and Villa routed the Colorados at the village of Bermejillo.

As Orozco retreated toward his main base, Chihuahua city, Huerta pressed northward, driving the Colorados without letup. Orozco destroyed the railroad as he retired, but this did not stop Huerta. Forcing his men to work around the clock, he repaired the track mile by mile until Orozco retreated up to the American border.

On July 3, 1912, a final battle was fought at Bechimba. The Red Flaggers were soundly beaten. Orozco fled to Ciudad Juarez and then sneaked over into the United States. Within a few weeks, the Orozco uprising was ended.

Huerta received a hero's welcome back in Mexico City. Stumbling drunkenly, peering blearily through his eyeglasses, Huerta was dined, wined, toasted, and feted. When he was called to account for nearly one million pesos missing from funds allotted him, Huerta was brought before a congressional committee. Hero or no hero, he was questioned sharply.

Losing his temper, Huerta shouted at his inquisitors, "I'm a soldier, damn you! I'm not a damned bookkeeper! I don't know and I don't care what happened to your money!" With that, he stormed out of the room, retired to the nearest bar, and drained a bottle of cognac.

Congress and Madero were in such awe of Huerta

that the general received a medal, a bejeweled sword, and a promotion to major general instead of being indicted for embezzling government funds.

- 13 -

THE PLOTTERS

During the first year of his presidency, Francisco Madero had scarcely known an hour's tranquillity. The country was in more of a muddle than ever. Madero's attempts at democracy had flopped. Turmoil, not democracy, held sway in Mexico. Two minor and one major rebellion had been crushed, but in Morelos Zapata still fought on for land and liberty.

Madero was hounded from every side. Big businessmen opposed him with all their power and influence. Their lackeys in Congress sabotaged every reform Madero proposed. Detested by business, Madero was also distrusted by the masses who had put him into office.

The people's basic needs—land, food, health care, jobs, and education—all of which Madero had promised, were not forthcoming. Madero's promises were proving to be empty ones, although it was not always his fault.

U.S. Ambassador Henry Lane Wilson wrote disparagingly of Madero: "His government is apathetic, ineffective and either indifferent or stupidly optimistic. One day, Madero is a conservative, a stern avenger of society against brigandage . . . and the next, an apostle of peace, a friend of the poor, apologist for bandits and criminals."

Wilson's behavior toward Madero was biased and undiplomatic. He did not like the Mexican president and never hesitated to show his feelings. An American newsman characterized Wilson's attitude as "one of a personal vendetta rather than national policy."

In 1910, when Henry Lane Wilson had first taken up his duties in Mexico, he was fifty-three years old, a career diplomat with a long record of service in Chile, Belgium, and elsewhere. He arrived in Mexico City during the great September festival of 1910. The splendor of the celebration impressed Wilson, as did Porfirio Diaz, whom he called "the architect of Mexican progress."

American businessmen made a point of wooing Wilson. He adopted their viewpoint completely and displayed partisan hostility toward the Madero government. The ambassador had done everything he could to crush the Madero insurrection and had tried to persuade President Taft that United States intervention was necessary "for the protection of American lives and property."

However, Taft did not fall for that and Wilson was forced to take another tack. He flooded the White House with reports stressing the "instability" and "weaknesses" of the Madero regime and also asserted that Madero, in his opinion, was unfit for the presidency and incapable of conducting executive work.

After Madero's inauguration, Wilson grew even more hostile to him. Had the Mexican president been a shrewd politician, he could have won Wilson with cajolery, flattery, and hypocrisy. But Madero was naïvely honest and made no effort to mask his antipathy for Wilson. As a result, the relationship between the ambassador and the president degenerated to the point of a cold politeness that barely coated their mutual ill will.

Wilson kept sniping away at Madero. His dispatches to Washington always contained something against

Madero and warned that Mexico was "seething with discontent." He sounded the alarm again and again that American lives and property were in peril because of the "unstable conditions" in Mexico.

In March 1912, Wilson called upon Washington for one thousand rifles and a million cartridges "to defend Americans in Mexico City." The United States government would not fill such a large arms order, but did send a more modest shipment of weapons to the American Embassy.

Madero became so annoyed at Wilson that after the United States presidential election of November 1912, when Woodrow Wilson—not related to the ambassador— was elected, the Mexican requested that the president-elect recall Ambassador Wilson.

But Woodrow Wilson would not be inaugurated until March 1913. Taft, nearing the end of his term, refused to relieve Ambassador Wilson; had he done so, it would have been an admission that his policy in Mexico was a failure. So Henry Lane Wilson stayed on in Mexico City and continued to subvert Madero.

Reports reaching President Madero indicated that new rebellions were being fostered. For his own reasons, Madero chose to disregard these allegations. He also rebuffed advisers who urged him to execute the imprisoned leaders of past insurrections. In January 1913, the Madero government held two traitorous generals—Bernardo Reyes and Felix Diaz, Porfirio's nephew. (Diaz had led an abortive uprising in October 1911. He briefly captured and held Veracruz, where he had been military commander. His uprising was short-lived and Maderistas took Diaz prisoner on October 23, 1911.)

A man more cold-blooded than Madero would have liquidated Reyes and Diaz. But Madero was reluctant to shoot anyone. This softheartedness evoked from a presidential aide an exasperated outburst: "Does anyone believe that a president who does not shoot, who does not punish, who does not make himself feared, who always invokes laws and principles, can preside? Madero is a good man. But it is not a good man that is now needed."

Madero was to suffer cruelly because he let his foes live. Granted clemency, Reyes and Diaz set up subversive shop in prison. They were permitted visitors, and a steady stream of army officers called upon them. The plotters could conspire against Madero without interference.

On February 4, 1913, an army officer disgruntled with his fellow conspirators revealed the officers' plot to Gustavo Madero and gave him a list of the leading rebels. Named on that paper were: Felix Diaz; Bernardo Reyes; his son, Rodolfo; General Manuel Mondragon; General Aureliano Blanquet; General Joaquin Beltran; General Rubio Navarrete; General Gregorio Ruiz; and General Victoriano Huerta. A question mark was penciled in next to Huerta's name.

Gustavo hastened to alert his brother at the National Palace. A little later, he came out, shaking his head. He told a friend, "I don't know what's wrong with Francisco. He simply won't believe there is a plot. He *won't* believe it! He says Blanquet and Beltran are loyal, that all the generals are loyal. The question mark after Huerta, he thinks, proves the list false. Because, he says, the only one who *would* plot against him is Huerta!"

Only a man as stubborn and gullible as Madero would have brushed off the evidence. At the least, he should have had the listed officers brought in for interrogation. Instead, he did nothing, blithely refusing to concede that there actually was a plot.

But a plot did exist and was well advanced when Gustavo got wind of it. According to the plan, Bernardo Reyes was to be proclaimed provisional president. As soon as possible after that, Felix Diaz would be declared president of the Republic and would serve out the remainder of the six-year term that his uncle, Porfirio Diaz, had begun in 1910.

General Mondragon was to be minister of war, Rodolfo Reyes minister of justice, and Huerta commander in chief of the army. The only reason a question mark had been placed after Huerta's name was because he objected to the distribution of governmental positions. He felt that neither Bernardo Reyes nor Diaz was fit for the presidency—the man for the job was Victoriano Huerta. His intransigence made some of his co-conspirators doubt Huerta. But the alcoholic general stayed with the conspiracy and finally agreed to the overall plan.

The plotters soon learned that their scheme had been leaked to Gustavo Madero and passed on to the president. They originally had scheduled the uprising for March 16, 1913, but were now forced to move earlier. Plans were reshuffled. And on Saturday, February 8, 1913, five weeks ahead of time, the signal for rebellion was given, though Mondragon could muster only eight hundred men, three batteries of artillery, and about six hundred military school cadets for a march on Mexico City. Mondragon had planned for a force almost twice as large but had to do with what he could pull together on short notice. His first objective on reaching Mexico City was to release Reyes and Diaz from their separate prisons.

Mondragon managed to execute this mission, although not without unpleasant incidents. At Santiago Tlaltelolco, where Reyes was incarcerated, the commandant was shot dead when he refused to release the prisoner. There also was some trouble at the Ciudadela, a barracks and arsenal, in which Diaz was confined. The commandant there would not let his prisoner go free and put up a fight that ended with his being thrown into a cell by the rebellious officers.

It was 2:00 A.M., Sunday, February 9, when the duty officer at the National Palace was alerted by the sound of marching troops. He telephoned Gustavo Madero and then roused out the guard. Gustavo, a hat jammed on his head, a cigar clenched between his teeth, eyes flashing behind his glasses, leaped into his automobile and raced to the palace.

There, a traitorous colonel named Morelos was at the main gate waiting to admit Mondragon. When Gustavo came up, Morelos ordered him arrested. But Gustavo, a dynamic orator, climbed to the roof of his car and called on the guard to defend the government. He was so eloquent that the soldiers arrested Morelos, set up machine guns on the roof of the palace, and deployed riflemen.

General Lauro Villar, commanding the Mexico City garrison, a loyal Maderista, left a sickbed to take command of the palace defenses. His men had barely been emplaced when Bernardo Reyes, escorted by two hundred cavalrymen, entered the Zocalo and headed for the palace gates. It was about 5:00 A.M.

Reyes was supposed to occupy the presidential suite and issue a manifesto proclaiming himself provisional president and announcing the overthrow of Madero. Reyes had expected the gates to be opened for him. Instead he was challenged so sharply that his troopers pulled up short. General Villar came out and warned Reyes to turn back or be shot.

Reyes was certain that Villar, an old friend, would not give an order to fire. "Stand aside, Lauro!" he cried. "Don't try to stop us!" He turned and signaled his column on. The cavalrymen moved slowly forward.

"Traitor!" Villar bellowed. "You've been warned! Open fire! *Open fire!*"

The guard responded at once. A rifle volley shattered the morning stillness. Bernardo Reyes toppled from his horse, riddled with bullets, an outstretched hand pointed at the palace and the presidential chair he had coveted for so long.

A few scattered shots came from the cavalrymen. Villar fell, seriously wounded. Machine guns went into action from the palace roof. Lead sprayed the Zocalo, killing or wounding many rebels but also causing casualties among onlookers who had paused on their way to early mass at the nearby cathedral.

The palace guard charged out into the Zocalo and insurrectos fled in every direction. Among the prisoners captured was grossly fat General Ruiz, the cavalry commander. He had been unhorsed and was taken as he tried to waddle away on foot.

When the shooting began, Felix Diaz and Mondragon, at the head of the six hundred cadets, had been marching to the Zocalo. The fleeing cavalry troopers ran into them and the rebels fled in disorder to the Ciudadela barracks about a mile from the palace.

Gustavo Madero, convinced that the rebellion had been crushed, so informed his brother by telephone. At the time, Francisco Madero was at a loyal army installation just outside Mexico City. The president hastily mobilized a large force of cavalry augmented by mounted police and hastened to the palace.

When he reached Alameda Park, a half mile from the palace, loyalists on duty warned him that snipers were firing sporadically around the Zocalo. Despite the danger, Madero rode ahead and was barely missed by a sniper's bullet near the Fine Arts Palace.

The bodies sprawled in the Zocalo convinced Madero that he faced a serious crisis. For once he acted with alacrity. Casting aside his usually gentle and philosophical manner, Madero took decisive measures. The treacherous Colonel Morelos and the paunchy General Ruiz were sentenced to death by firing squad and the sentences were carried out. This time Madero was showing no mercy.

The rebellion seemed to have petered out except for mopping-up operations. However, the wound suffered by General Villar all but negated the government's initial successes. Had Villar been able to retain command, Madero's forces in Mexico City would easily have liquidated the resistance of the rebels holed up in the Ciudadela. But Villar's disabling wound made necessary the calling of another general to carry on the final suppression of the rebellion.

Under usual circumstances Villar would have been replaced by General Felipe Angeles, a dedicated Maderista and one of Mexico's best soldiers. Angeles would have made short shrift of the insurrectos. But he was not then available. He was off in Morelos fighting Zapata and could not be reached in time.

The only ranking general in Mexico City was Victoriano Huerta. However, Madero suspected him now, even though Huerta had not taken part in the uprising. Only after some painful soul-searching and discussion with his cabinet did Madero agree to let Huerta command the government forces.

Stone sober for a change, Huerta was summoned before the president and told what was expected of him. The general swore his unswerving loyalty to Madero. So sincere were his avowals that Madero, always ready to trust a man, gave the general a hearty abrazo and put his fate in Huerta's hands. For Madero, that abrazo was the embrace of death.

- 14 -

"MY PLACE IS HERE!"

In 1913, Victoriano Huerta was fifty-nine years old. Born of poor parents in Jalisco, he was befriended by wealthy townspeople who were impressed by his intelligence and diligence as he scurried about doing odd jobs to earn money for his family. Huerta's patrons sponsored his education and then helped put him through the military academy, from which he graduated with top honors. He rose rapidly in the army during the Diaz regime and was a brigadier general by 1910.

People had strong feelings about Huerta, but there was no unanimity of opinion. Some saw him as a brilliant officer and a sincere patriot. Others regarded him as cold, ambitious, and untrustworthy.

One historian has said: "Huerta was a villain on a grand scale. An able general possessed of a masterful and magnetic personality, he was also a drunkard and a man for whom honor did not exist. From the moment he was appointed general of government troops during the 1913 uprising, he resolved both to ensure the triumph of the rebellion and to maneuver himself to the head of it."

Placing Huerta in command of government forces in Mexico City was another of Madero's incomprehensible acts. When Villar fell wounded, Huerta got the chance he had been seeking for years. He used it with a frightening combination of skill, double-crossing, and viciousness seldom matched in his country's history. Huerta purposely subjected Mexico City to a period of wanton killings, terror, and anguish to achieve his ends. The terrible time was fittingly known as the Ten Tragic Days.

A man with Huerta's military abilities was not needed to finish off the rebels in the Ciudadela. Any competent officer could have done that. Diaz, General Mondragon, and their dispirited men could easily have been shelled out of the stronghold in a few hours with a minimum of bloodshed.

But Diaz and Huerta had been in collusion from the outset. According to plan, both sides opened a steady artillery bombardment. Shells exploded everywhere but on the main targets—the Ciudadela and the National Palace. During all the shooting, only two shells ever hit the Ciudadela and one struck the palace.

The guns pounded away incessantly. Shells burst in the business and residential districts, causing widespread damage, starting fires, killing and wounding civilians everywhere in Mexico City. Any neighborhood within artillery range was endangered. The purpose of the generals was to panic the populace and shatter the people's faith in the government. Once this had taken place, the traitors reasoned, the masses would be glad to accept a "strong man" to restore order.

Compounding the confusion and chaos, the rebels opened Belem prison, liberating hundreds of criminals and felons. These lawbreakers scattered throughout the city and loosed a tidal wave of crime.

With criminals at large, shells exploding, fires raging, and death on every side, Madero decided that Mexico City needed reinforcements. Leaving Huerta in full charge, the president set out for Cuernavaca to bring back General Angeles and several trusted regiments. Madero and his party arrived safely in Cuernavaca on February 11.

General Angeles reluctantly agreed to release two thousand men for duty in Mexico City and to accompany the troops. He returned with Madero the following day. The last man Huerta wanted in the capital was General Angeles. The loyal officer sized up the situation almost immediately and asked pointed questions about the unrelenting artillery duel. But before he could get too troublesome, Huerta, the ranking commander, ordered Angeles and his men out of the city to cover the approaches from Morelos as a security precaution in case Zapata attacked.

Fuming, Angeles had no recourse except to obey. At the moment, Madero would accept no criticism of Huerta. Once again the little president had been duped by a traitorous enemy. So Angeles marched away, awaiting a Zapatista offensive he knew would never come.

In Mexico City, Diaz and Huerta played out their deadly farce. The civilian population grew more desperate every hour. Guns boomed, shells crashed, and death struck down men, women, and children, rich and poor alike.

The city lay paralyzed. Corpses were piled in the streets—how many, nobody knew. Food and medical supplies ran out. Water was shut off. There was neither gas nor electricity. Housewives, braving the rain of steel, scurried about buying up all the food in sight. Pedestrians, carrying white flags made of torn bed sheets nailed to broomsticks, hurried through the ruined streets. But the truce flags did not help. Trigger-happy snipers shot down anyone they saw.

As fighting went on, day after bloodstained day, the foreigners in Mexico City armed themselves. Rifle-toting civilians patrolled the neighborhoods. Looters were killed on the spot. The foreigners were ready to fight either rebels or loyalists.

Meanwhile, the shelling continued. A battalion of troops especially loyal to Madero was ordered by Huerta to mount a frontal assault on the Ciudadela. The soldiers bravely charged across open ground and were mowed down by machine guns. That battalion never saw combat again. Too few had survived the murderous fire.

After this debacle, a member of the Japanese legation came secretly to Gustavo Madero. He told the president's brother that within a day's time he could mobilize two thousand Japanese residents of the city, disguise them as peons, and, arming them with knives only, make a night attack on the Ciudadela. They would murder the defenders and crush the rebellion in a single night. Gustavo haughtily turned down this bloodthirsty offer, stating that Mexicans could fight their own battles.

Representatives of the diplomatic corps raced back and forth through the streets, their cars flying British, French, German, Japanese, or American flags, as ambassadors and consuls tried to negotiate a cease-fire. The efforts were to no avail. Neither Diaz nor Huerta thought the time was right to call off the mock hostilities.

The cannonading was intensified on February 14 and 15, adding hundreds of civilians to casualty lists. As the ordeal continued, U.S. Ambassador Wilson made a decisive move. He called a meeting of the entire diplomatic corps at the American Embassy on February 15. The purpose was to draw up a statement calling for Madero to resign and delegate his powers to Congress. With shells bursting and windows shattering, the diplomats agreed to present such a demand to the president.

A Spanish diplomat brought the message to Madero, who ordered the Spaniard out of his office and sent an angry cable to Washington complaining that Wilson was interfering in Mexico's domestic affairs. But indignation could not stave off the collapse of the Madero government. After nine days of around-the-clock shelling, the people of Mexico City were ready for any measures that would end the drawn-out agony. Huerta confidently told a foreign diplomat to expect Madero's downfall at any hour. The imminence of this was admitted by all except Madero himself.

Interviewed in the National Palace by a British journalist, he responded to a question about his rumored resignation. Emphatically, he said: "These rumors have no foundation. I have never for a moment entertained the idea. . . . I was elected by the people of Mexico in a free and untrammeled vote. . . . I intend to be faithful to the trust committed to me by the people and the nation, though it may cost me my life."

Stressing his words, Madero clenched his fists and pounded on the arms of the chair in which he was seated. "My place is here! *Here!*" he cried.

The interview appeared on February 18, Madero's last day as president. That morning, suspicious at last of General Huerta, Madero had decided to replace him with General Aureliano Blanquet, commanding the Twenty-ninth Brigade, an elite force of four thousand men. Blanquet was ordered to move the Twenty-ninth

Brigade into Mexico City and to assume the defense of the palace. Madero seemed to have forgotten that Blanquet's name had been on the list of conspirators—without a question mark after it.

Shortly after noon, February 18, Blanquet, wearing a dress uniform and all his decorations, appeared before Madero, accompanied by several officers. In a firm, steady voice Blanquet bluntly told Madero that the only salvation for the country was the president's resignation.

"I have come to insist that you step down at once," Blanquet said.

Just as bluntly, Madero refused. Blanquet whipped out a pistol and leveled it at the president. "You are my prisoner!" he snapped.

Madero's bodyguards went for their side arms. Shots were exchanged. Several men fell dead. A scuffle ensued. In a few seconds it was all over. Madero was led away in handcuffs, under military arrest. Within a few hours, the Madero administration was no more, betrayed and destroyed by men who abhorred the least degree of democracy and political freedom.

- 15 -

"ADIOS, MY GENERAL"

Shortly after the president was arrested, the cabinet and Madero's brother, Gustavo, also were taken into custody. General Huerta moved swiftly following the arrests. Setting himself up in the National Palace, he sent messengers to the Ciudadela to advise Diaz of the coup. Huerta then reached all state governors by telegram. "I have assumed charge of the government. . . . Madero and his cabinet are prisoners in my power," he declared.

Late in the afternoon of February 18, Huerta and Diaz appeared on a balcony of the palace. Huerta told a cheering crowd, "Mexicans! Brothers! There will be no more shelling! Peace has come!"

The people in the Zocalo yelled and applauded. At the moment, it made no difference who sat in the president's chair. The only thing that counted was an end to the shooting.

Henry Lane Wilson had played something more than the role of a neutral diplomat amid the intrigue and treachery that had brought on Madero's downfall. He could not conceal his delight at Madero's fate. The ambassador gave wholehearted support to Diaz and Huerta. Indeed, that very evening he had a champagne buffet at the American Embassy for all members of the diplomatic corps to witness Huerta and Diaz signing a peace pact.

That night Wilson told his guests, "Mexico is saved. From now on we shall have peace, progress, and prosperity!" He then proposed a toast to Diaz and Huerta, calling them the "saviors of Mexico."

Before the festivities were ended Huerta was appointed provisional president, despite some mild objections from backers of the late Bernardo Reyes, who preferred Diaz. However, an agreement was reached. With Huerta as interim president, Diaz was free "to pursue his candidacy for the presidency."

The next day, Wednesday, February 19, Huerta announced his cabinet. Several men left over from the days of Porfirio Diaz were included: Francisco de la Barra was foreign minister; General Manuel Mondragon, minister of war; Rodolfo Reyes, minister of justice. The remainder of the posts were doled out to supporters of Reyes and Felix Diaz.

Once the cabinet appointments were made public, the arrested members of Madero's cabinet were released from custody. At Huerta's request they all resigned except Pedro Lescurain, the foreign minister; according to the constitution, he was in line to succeed Madero.

Since Huerta wanted to please world opinion by following the constitution, he next asked for the resignations of Madero and Vice-President Jose Pino Suarez. Both agreed to comply after receiving the promise that they would get safe passage out of Mexico with their families.

Lescurain brought the signed resignations to Huerta, but before handing them over begged the general to spare the lives of Madero and Pino Suarez. Huerta said, "Whatever you ask." With a sudden gesture, he took from beneath his shirt a medal of the Virgin of Guadalupe, Mexico's patron saint, on a golden chain. Kissing the medal, he vowed, "I swear to you that I shall permit no one to make an attempt against the lives of Senor Madero and Senor Pino Suarez."

This was good enough for Lescurain, a devout Catholic. He handed over the resignations and left Huerta, convinced that no harm would befall Madero or Pino Suarez.

That night, an emergency session of Congress overwhelmingly accepted the resignations. Under the constitution, Lescurain succeeded to the presidency, which he held exactly twenty-six minutes, just long enough to appoint Huerta minister of the interior, the office next in line for the presidency. Lescurain then resigned and Huerta took over.

The trappings of constitutionality had been adhered to, but few people were fooled. Huerta was president, not through any democratic process, but by force and trickery. The country received a sample of what might be expected from the new regime when Huerta sent a telegram to state governors saying: *"Accept my authority or perish!"* These were scarcely the words and sentiments of an avowed follower of the constitution.

The true face of the Diaz-Huerta rebellion was apparent in a tragedy being enacted at the Ciudadela at the very moment Congress was taking its vote on Madero's resignation. The president's brother, Gustavo, then being held captive in the National Palace, was removed under strong guard to the Ciudadela. The escort set him free in the barracks courtyard. As Gustavo walked away, his guards shot him down. As usual, the official explanation was "shot while trying to escape"—the *ley fuga*.

That same busy evening, February 19, arrangements were being made to send Madero, Pino Suarez, and their families to Veracruz by train, there to board ship for Europe. A special two-carriage train was waiting at Buena Vista station for a scheduled midnight departure. Long before that time, Senora Madero, Senora Pino Suarez, and members of the two families were on board —bag and baggage.

But at 2:00 A.M., the worried families were removed from the train. The order for taking Madero and Pino Suarez to Veracruz had been countermanded by Huerta. He had learned that the army commander in Veracruz was an ardent Maderista and was planning to free the deposed president upon his arrival at the port. Huerta was taking no chances. He did not want to face a Maderista uprising in Veracruz or anywhere else.

The ex-president and vice-president were held under strict security in the National Palace until late at night on February 22. Then Madero and Pino Suarez were told they were being moved from the National Palace to the city penitentiary. General Felipe Angeles, whom Huerta had arrested for his loyalty to Madero, shared the room in the palace with the president and Pino Suarez. As

Madero and his companion were being led from the chamber, the ex-president turned to Angeles with tears in his eyes. "Adios, my general. I shall never see you again," he said in a husky whisper.

At 11:15 P.M., the palace gates swung open and two cars lurched out. Madero was in one, Pino Suarez in the other, both heavily guarded. Reporters waiting outside the palace tried to follow the autos on foot, but were quickly left behind.

The local correspondent of the *New York World* was hurrying toward the city penitentiary, the direction the autos had taken. As he neared the building, he heard a dozen or so shots. Running, he reached the gate and asked a policeman what had happened.

"Madero and Pino Suarez have been shot dead! Some men tried to rescue them," the officer said. According to later testimony by Captain Francisco Cardenas, commanding the guard detail, the two cars had been fired upon by a group of men lying in ambush near the prison. Cardenas claimed that both Madero and Pino Suarez had leaped out of their cars and run toward the ambushers. "They were caught in the cross fire and killed," Cardenas blandly explained.

Few swallowed the Cardenas story after an autopsy revealed that Madero had been killed by a single bullet at the base of the skull, fired from close range. It was rumored that Huerta had ordered the two men killed, but no evidence actually linking him to the murders ever was unearthed.

Captain Cardenas was promoted to major after his failure to safeguard Madero. "Huerta has a rather peculiar way of punishing a man who flubbed his job," the *World* correspondent wrote.

Although Huerta promised an immediate and full investigation, none was ever held. Madero was dead at thirty-nine, an idealist unable to cope with ruthless enemies. He had held office only briefly—fifteen months. As one historian commented, "He was not a Strong Man with capital letters. Had he followed the Diaz dictum, 'Better shed bad blood now than good blood later,' he might have survived . . . for he would have had Felix Diaz and his fellow conspirators executed while there still was time."

But Madero was a compassionate man, a man of magnanimity and a love for legal processes. Many mistook these traits for weakness rather than idealism. He never had a chance to put his program in effect. Mexican and foreign landowners had fought him; they were helped by a hostile press that leveled venom at the man who had granted it the freedom of criticism. Madero never knuckled under to the American ambassador, Henry Lane Wilson, nor did he give in to the generals who disliked him. Ironically, his greatest failing was his sincerity.

"Considering everything, it was a wonder that Madero managed to accomplish anything at all," a historian wrote. "The fall of the Madero government was a national disaster regardless of the merits of the government itself. Those who were responsible . . . had no substitute acceptable to the nation. Nothing was gained by the overthrow of Madero."

PART

III

The Strong Man

"I AM READY
TO MAKE WAR ON YOU!"

Madero's enemies and the followers of Porfirio Diaz were delighted when Huerta took power. They believed that the hard-drinking general was the "strong man" Mexico had been lacking since Diaz's downfall. Landowners, church, army, foreign investors, bankers, and businessmen rallied to Huerta. Pascual Orozco and his Colorados swore fealty to the new regime. So enthused were Huerta's admirers that a cigarette manufacturer printed the general's picture on cards distributed with every pack.

Kaiser William II of Germany, who also fancied himself a strong man, was impressed by the way Huerta had taken over. The Kaiser cabled Huerta, praising a "brave soldier who dared save his country with the sword of honor." A newspaper tagged Huerta with the nickname "the Mexican Cromwell." Ambassador Henry Lane Wilson went further than most Huerta fans. The ambassador was literally hypnotized by him and did everything possible to gain Washington's recognition of Huerta. He assured President Taft, now in his last weeks as chief executive, that the general was accepted wholeheartedly by all Mexico.

However, Wilson was bending the truth. Proof of this came from Coahuila state where Venustiano Carranza, the governor, cabled Taft: "The Mexican peo-

ple condemn the villainous *coup d'état* which deprived
Mexico of her constitutional rulers by cowardly assassination. . . . I am certain that your government as well
as that of your successor will not accept the spurious
government which Huerta is attempting to establish."

This protest was closely followed by a report from
the United States consul in Sonora, who said: "The majority of the people in Sonora do not favor Huerta." A
day or two later, Washington was informed that the state
of Coahuila was in revolt.

The Coahuila uprising shook Huerta less than did
the removal of Henry Lane Wilson as ambassador to
Mexico by Woodrow Wilson after his inauguration on
March 4, 1913. President Wilson clearly stated that he
would not recognize Huerta and indicated that he believed the general to be a usurper and a murderer. Apparently Wilson intended to make an example of Huerta
in an effort to stop the revolts and insurrections that
had plagued Latin Americans for so long. By showing
American disapproval of men who gained power forcibly,
President Wilson hoped to win support for bringing governmental changes about through democratic processes.
This attitude made Huerta's position difficult, but the general's greatest problem was the resistance that rose to
oppose him within Mexico.

It soon became apparent that this opposition would
be formidable. In Morelos, Zapata fought Huerta even
harder than he had battled Porfirio Diaz and Madero.
The Zapatistas hated Huerta with good reason. In the
early days of the Madero regime, he had hunted them
down.

As always, the hub of rebellion was in the north.
Venustiano Carranza, an unlikely revolutionary, was the
main figure of the anti-Huerta movement. Like Madero,
Carranza owned land, but he did not come close to equal-
ing the murdered president's wealth. During the Diaz
regime, Carranza had served twelve years as a senator

from Coahuila. He had become disenchanted with Diaz and in 1910 joined the Madero Revolution. Tall and dignified, Carranza wore blue-tinted glasses to protect his weak eyes. His long white beard gave him the appearance of "a biblical prophet," according to one observer. A decent man basically, Carranza was conceited and believed that he was "incapable of making a mistake." He felt that only he could save Mexico from the "plague" of Huertism.

Speaking of Carranza, a historian has noted: "It was ironical that this self-complacent country squire should have become the spokesman of the anti-Huerta resistance. Carranza had substantial virtues. He was financially honest and had no love for bloodshed. Unfortunately, he was domineering, egotistical, and remarkably ignorant of the history and needs of the people whom he proposed to govern."

On March 26, 1913, at the Hacienda de Guadalupe, Carranza openly called for rebellion against Huerta and published the Plan of Guadalupe, a vague, ambiguous document acceptable to all groups of anti-Huertistas. The Plan called for the appointment of the fifty-four-year-old Carranza as "First Chief" of the Constitutionalists, the name given his movement because it sought to restore constitutionality in Mexico.

Carranza's choice of a name for his revolution was a fortunate one. President Woodrow Wilson was favorably impressed by the word *constitutionalist*. To him it smacked of democracy, which was the keystone of Wilson's political philosophy. The American president was convinced that the oppressed Mexican people had found a genuine champion in Carranza.

However, the Carranza rebellion, although highly principled, got off on the wrong foot. Carranza was no military man and, as a result, chose an inept commander for his forces in Coahuila. He picked General Pablo Gonzalez, an officer who reputedly had never won a battle in his life. Fortunately, not all Carranza's generals were like Gonzalez.

In the state of Sonora, the anti-Huerta campaign was led by Alvaro Obregon—a man who one day would be president of Mexico. Obregon had merry, twinkling eyes, a ready smile, an uptilted nose, and ruddy cheeks, resembling an Irishman more than a Mexican. The youngest of eighteen children, he learned to read and write in the local school at Alamos, Sonora, where he was born in 1880. He started working as an apprentice mechanic on a hacienda at the age of thirteen.

But by the time the Madero Revolution broke out in 1910, Obregon had laid down his mechanic's tools and had become a prosperous farmer raising chick-peas on a plot of land near the Sonoran village of Huatabampo. Married, he had several children and was so well thought of in Huatabampo that the villagers elected him mayor.

Obregon had taken no part in the Madero uprising. Although a Maderista at heart, he was reluctant to shoulder a rifle and fight for the cause.

But when Orozco and his Colorados had risen against Madero in 1912, Obregon could stay on the sidelines no longer. He recruited a force of some three hundred fairly well-to-do farmers into what was known as the "Rich Man's Battalion" and rode off at their head to battle the detested Colorados.

When the anti-Huerta movement got under way, Obregon and his men took to the field again. An avowed socialist, Obregon was an unusual commander. He surrounded himself with a competent and intelligent staff. His every move was thoroughly discussed with them. In a succession of well-handled campaigns, Obregon routed the Huertista forces and soon controlled much of Sonora state, giving the Constitutionalists a good base easily accessible to sources of arms in the United States.

Huerta reluctantly wrote off Sonora, but moved swiftly to hold Chihuahua. He arrested the pro-Madero governor, Abraham Gonzalez, and replaced him with a staunch Huertista, General Antonio Rabago. To make sure that Gonzalez would give no trouble, Huerta had him moved by train from prison in Chihuahua city to a Mexico City jail. When the train stopped to take on water at an obscure station, Gonzalez was "shot while trying to escape" and buried beside the track in an unmarked grave.

However, the slaying did not go unobserved. A peon witnessed the crime and passed his information to Pancho Villa, who was in hiding on the American side of the Rio Grande because Huerta had placed a price on his head. When he learned that Gonzalez had been murdered, Villa flew into a rage. Calming down, he decided that his place was in Mexico, not skulking in Texas.

Accompanied by eight comrades, Villa stole horses from an El Paso livery stable and crossed the shallow Rio Grande to Mexico. Once back on his native soil, he sent a telegram to General Rabago in his customary flamboyant style: "I am now in Mexico. I am ready to make war on you!"

- 17 -

"NOT COLLEAGUES BUT ACCOMPLICES"

General Antonio Rabago, the governor of Chihuahua, was shaken by Villa's telegram. The last thing the general wanted was to tangle with Villa, so he came up with a proposition for the tough outlaw chief. The general

115

reached Villa through an emissary and offered him a purse of 100,000 pesos plus command of a division with the rank of major general if he joined Huerta.

Villa replied, "I refuse your bribes. Tell Huerta I don't need rank—I already command free men. As for money, tell the bald-headed goat to spend it on brandy!"

Setting up camp in the rugged Chihuahua hills, Villa sent out a call for men. The peons came to him, moving like ragged shadows through mountain draws and passes. They quit haciendas, mines, mills, factories, towns, and small villages, drawn by the magic of Villa's name. They came singly, by twos, tens, twenties, and fifties; old men and young ones; robust girls and withered old ladies. Some carried weapons, a motley assortment of arms to pit against Mausers, Maxims, and artillery, but they came without fear, ready to give their lives because Villa had sent for them.

And with the ragtag volunteers came swarms of women and children. Women—both on the rebel and the federal side—had always played an important part in Mexican armies. They served as cooks, laundresses, and nurses. They shared the rigors and hardships of battle with the men, sometimes on the firing line, earning the title *soldaderas*, woman soldiers. To one observer, Villa's army seemed more like "a migration of refugees than a military force." He was referring to the pots, pans, bedding, and personal belongings the women brought to the encampment.

Villa turned to an old fund-raising standby to raise money for guns and ammunition—cattle rustling. He and his men stole thousands of cattle from the huge Chihuahua haciendas, drove the herds north to Texas, sold them, and used the cash for weapons.

When he had about seven hundred armed men, Villa launched his first campaign. His target was Casas Grandes, which had seen fighting in 1910. About four hundred Colorados were garrisoned at Casas Grandes,

116

and Pancho Villa meant business when he attacked. After a clash lasting more than two hours, the Villistas took the town. The Colorados fled in disorder, leaving forty dead and sixty prisoners, some of them wounded.

Villa had warned that the Red Flaggers could expect no mercy, and he kept his word. Prisoners were lined up three deep and shot. Villa had decided to save ammunition by having one bullet kill three men. He had won an impressive victory; but at the same time he set the standard for the cruelties that were to mark the course of Carranza's Revolution.

Venustiano Carranza, First Chief of the Constitutionalists, became aware that in Pancho Villa he had a valuable ally. The First Chief paid a visit to Villa, seeking from him a pledge of support for the Plan of Guadalupe. Pancho readily agreed to this; he would have agreed to any movement opposing Huerta. He also saluted Carranza as First Chief.

Thus started a strange relationship, one forged by the demands of the moment, not based on friendship or even mutual regard. It was farfetched that Carranza, the suave, urbane, and dignified landowner, could find any common ground with Pancho Villa, an earthy, passionate, and semiliterate peon. But the times required an alliance between these two men of opposite tastes and backgrounds. Villa served Carranza well during the period the union lasted.

As the struggle between Huerta and Carranza was shaping up, spring and summer passed with only minor fighting. Huerta kept trying desperately to win the backing of the United States. He did everything to persuade President Wilson that his administration deserved American recognition.

But Wilson was not buying Huerta. The deaths of Madero, Pino Suarez, and Abraham Gonzalez turned the American president against the general. Wilson was a stubborn man who rarely accepted anyone's advice and

117

had low regard for those whose opinions differed from his. Thus, when he was besieged by appeals from American businessmen in Mexico to recognize Huerta, Wilson doggedly refused to do so. He once told an aide: "I am the president of the whole United States, not merely a few property owners in Mexico. They might like Huerta, but I do not, and I will act in a manner to benefit the country, not the big business interests south of the border."

Despite the difficulties he was encountering from the American president, Huerta moved to consolidate his power. The first step he took was to dump cabinet ministers who might pose a threat to him. Within a few weeks of his take-over, he forced the resignations of the minister of education and the minister of interior, men whose political leanings did not quite match his.

Minister of War General Manuel Mondragon was next to go. Huerta feared Mondragon's influence among army officers. After a banquet attended by Huerta and Mondragon, the general was placed aboard a train heading north and advised not to return.

Huerta next sent Felix Diaz on a goodwill trip to Japan. Foreign Minister Francisco de la Barra was assigned as Mexico's ambassador to France. By summer's end, every cabinet member of any stature had been replaced by a Huerta stooge. According to one observer, "Huerta sought not colleagues but accomplices."

Huerta certainly turned out to be an unorthodox president. He rarely could be found in the National Palace. When he was needed, scouts were sent to scour saloons and cafés in search of him. In Mexico City, his favorite hangout was a tearoom called El Globo. There he would sit for hours, sipping cognac out of a teacup, slowly getting drunk. He passed his time matching coins with the pretty young cashier to see who should pay for his drinks. When the girl lost, the owner picked up the tab. Huerta was a good attraction for the place.

Cabinet meetings were conducted at the Bar Colon,

a rather disreputable place. Huerta frequently kept his advisers up until three or four o'clock in the morning while he went over affairs of state, draining a bottle of cognac at the same time.

An American businessman has recalled attending a meeting in Huerta's house during which the Mexican led him to a bookcase filled with impressively bound volumes. Huerta opened the bookcase door, pulled out a few books, and showed the American shelves filled with bottles of liquor. "These are the books that make my heart merry," Huerta chuckled.

On July 4, 1913, American residents of Mexico City invited Huerta to their traditional Independence Day party at the swank Tivoli Hotel. Dressed in a wrinkled gray business suit, his hat pulled down low, Huerta slipped past the official reception committee waiting for him at the entrance of the Tivoli without anyone recognizing him. A little later, someone spotted him drinking cognac in the hotel bar and hurried to tell the committeemen. The group hurried over to Huerta. He had finished off half the bottle of cognac and grinned at his hosts, "That's damned fine stuff. Far better than I can afford."

- 18 -

"GET OUT OF MY COUNTRY!"

In the summer of 1913, the backers of Carranza had reason to feel optimistic about the eventual outcome of their Revolution. Things were going well except in Coahuila, where bumbling General Pablo Gonzalez kept losing

119

one battle after the other. After the state capital, Saltillo, fell to the Huertistas in August, Carranza had to move his headquarters.

He set up a new one in Hermosillo, Sonora, where Huerta was no threat. Protected by Alvaro Obregon's followers, Carranza felt secure. He promptly promoted Obregon to brigadier general, but Carranza had not made much of an impression on him. "Carranza is a great man for little things and a small one for great things," Obregon told an aide.

With Carranza in Hermosillo playing at being First Chief, Pancho Villa pursued the war in Chihuahua. His bobtail army swarmed southward, growing in numbers as it marched. Independent outlaw bands, each with its own leader, joined Villa. He had reunions with men whom he had known in his own cattle-rustling, bandit days. Tomas Urbina emerged from Villa's past and brought with him six hundred men plus wagons loaded with booty taken from the town of Durango that he had sacked on the way to meet Villa. Unable to read or write, Urbina was known as "the Lion of Sierras," but he was an ailing and aging lion. Years of outlawry and hiding out in the mountains had left him almost crippled with rheumatism.

Urbina led some hard, cruel men. In that tough band few could match Fausto Borunda for sheer viciousness. Borunda was known as "the Matador" because he always killed prisoners. During the sacking of Durango, only a few federal soldiers had been taken captive. Borunda was sorely disappointed at not filling his blood quota. He made the rounds of cantinas and saloons, picked anyone who caught his attention, and asked whether the man was a Huerta sympathizer. If the answer was negative, Borunda shot the victim for lying. He kept up this murderous sport until it bored him.

Also riding with Urbina was a man named Rodolfo Fierro. In comparison to him, Borunda was mild. Nicknamed *El Carnicero*, "the Butcher," Fierro had the dubious distinction of being considered the most vicious killer in the ranks of the revolutionary forces. Tall, powerfully built, and heavily moustached, Fierro once personally executed three hundred captured Colorados. During this slaughter, he had to stop and massage his trigger finger, which had developed a cramp.

That summer of 1913, Villa's urgent call brought out other old war-horses. Maclovio Herrera, the Parral miner who had fought for Madero, came to Villa with four hundred miners, each a dynamite expert. These *dinamiteros* went into action smoking cigars, lighting dynamite fuses from the glowing butts, and hurling the explosive sticks like hand grenades.

Toribio Ortega, a Chihuahua cattleman, was a totally different sort of man than Urbina, Fierro, and Borunda. Known as "the Honorable One" because he never killed prisoners, Ortega had fought for La Revolucion and deeply believed in democracy and social justice. Unlike the others, he never took a penny for himself from revolutionary funds. "I am a rich man. Use the money to buy bread for the children of the poor," he said.

A half-dozen more independents latched onto Villa and soon he commanded more than eight thousand rebels. Although his was a loosely knit army, casually disciplined, poorly trained, and indifferently armed, Villa and his commanders decided, at the end of September, that they were in shape to undertake a major operation. Their objective was the vital communications center of Torreon in southwestern Coahuila. According to an American who owned a ranch near Torreon, the town was "misbegotten on an arid site for no better reason than that of the intersection of the railway lines, north and south, east and west."

According to the rancher, Torreon was "unpiped, undrained, unpaved, unrefrigerated . . . life's utmost luxury was that of window screening against flies by day and mosquitoes by night."

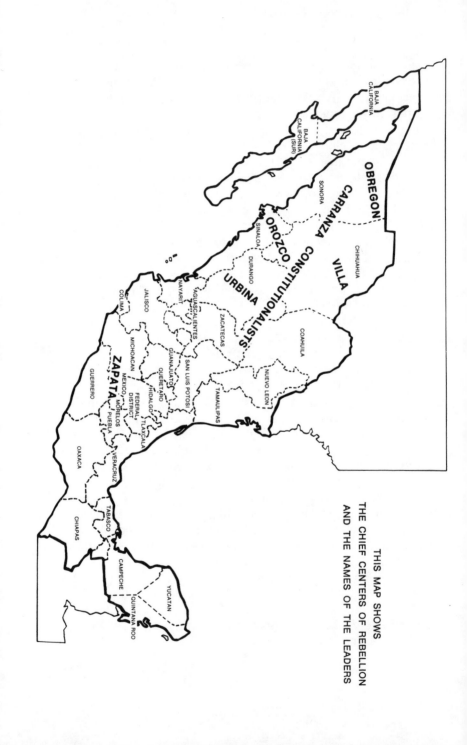

THIS MAP SHOWS
THE CHIEF CENTERS OF REBELLION
AND THE NAMES OF THE LEADERS

It was an unattractive place even by the lowest standards. But the town straddled the main railroad line in the midst of a heavily populated area. Its capture would cut the supply route to Mexico City and isolate federal troops in the north. Although Torreon was heavily defended, Villa felt that an attack on the town was a justifiable risk.

On September 29, before proceeding to the assault, Villa called all his commanders together at a hacienda near Torreon and asked them to elect a supreme commander. "One voice must speak for all. One set of orders must apply for all. One chief must command all," he said. The vote was swift and conclusive. Those present unanimously chose Villa. His first act was to dignify his motley army with the title Division of the North, a military designation that seemed overly formal for such an armed horde.

But the Division of the North, proud of its new name, shambled on to Torreon. According to Villa's scouts, the town was held by two thousand Federalistas, several hundred Colorados, and an assorted group of seven hundred volunteers—ranchers, cowboys, factory workers, railroad men, and wealthy Spaniards. The scouts warned Villa to expect hard fighting. The Colorados would put up especially fierce resistance; they knew that Fierro was with the attackers. No Red Flagger would surrender easily to El Carnicero. For a few days, sharp skirmishing took place in the vicinity of Torreon, but nothing important happened.

The battle around Torreon was conducted in an unmilitary manner. A British journalist with Villa was astounded by the informality of the officers and men. While a band played airs from *Carmen,* soldiers of the Division of the North strolled about in groups, pausing now and then to kneel and fire at the enemy. From time to time, they would form small bunches to charge a position. They seemed to have little regard for their own lives and were absolutely fearless. The Englishman later said, "Men such as these, properly trained, led, and armed, could whip any army in the world! I have never seen such raw courage!"

Fighting in this haphazard manner, the Division of the North reached the outskirts of Torreon on the evening of October 1. Under the cover of darkness, Villa consolidated his forces and, at midnight, led an overwhelming mass assault that swept down on the federals from three sides.

Fierce hand-to-hand fighting swirled for hours until the outnumbered defenders began pulling out of Torreon. They retreated eastward across the flooded Rio Nazas, crossing on bridges that they blew up after them. The destruction of the spans hampered pursuit, and at daybreak Villa declared the battle of Torreon officially ended.

It had been quite a night for Villa. Between darkness and daybreak, the Division of the North had captured the most important communications center in all northern Mexico, and had done so with remarkably few casualties. A large amount of war matériel was taken as well. The booty included a three-inch railway artillery cannon promptly called *El Niño*—the infant—because it was so large. Many shells for *El Niño* also were captured, along with 600 hand grenades, 1,000 rifles, 500,000 cartridges, and 6 new Maxim machine guns. As a special bonus, the Villistas also took 40 railway engines and more than 200 railroad cars.

With Torreon in his hands, Villa played conqueror to the beaten foe. But first he looked after the needs of his own men. Some of the captured railway cars were converted into a rolling hospital staffed with volunteer doctors and nurses. However, Villa's beneficence extended only to his people. He ordered all federal officers who had been taken prisoner to be shot. Prisoners of other ranks he gave a chance to switch sides.

He also raised eyebrows in the United States by confiscating some two million pesos from Torreon banks and distributing them to the poor of that town and neighboring communities. But Villa aroused the most unfavorable comment by his treatment of Torreon's Spanish residents. Because he believed that all Spaniards in Mexico supported Huerta—and most did—Villa acted harshly toward them. "I have one thing to tell you people. Get out of my country!" he bellowed at a group of frightened Spaniards gathered in the main square of Torreon. When foreign journalists protested that he was being unfair, Villa snapped, "I'm doing to the Spaniards what they've done to Mexicans for centuries."

Whether Villa was being just or unjust remains academic. He confiscated all property belonging to Torreon's Spanish community and gave the people forty-eight hours to get out of town or stay and be killed.

- 19 -

"MEXICO IS VERY SICK"

Losing Torreon added substantially to Huerta's problems. He was awash in a sea of adversity. Political foes were beginning to speak against him. A few days after the fall of Torreon, a well-known senator, speaking in the Chamber of Deputies, loosed a blistering attack on Huerta, denouncing him as "a dictator more pernicious than Porfirio Diaz."

When Huerta kept this speech out of the Chamber's official journal, the senator, Dr. Belisario Dominguez, printed it up in pamphlet form at his own expense and distributed the booklet throughout Mexico City. General Huerta was not a man to brook such defiance. One night, Dr. Dominguez was taken from his home by secret police and carted off to parts unknown. A week later, a goatherd found the senator's bullet-riddled body lying in a ditch some miles from the capital.

This killing stirred up a furor. The murder of Dominguez was discussed and argued in cafes, bars, cantinas, and restaurants. Few doubted that Huerta had ordered the shooting, but almost no one dared make that charge. Huerta's secret agents circulated in all public places. An incautious remark overheard might well bring arrest, torture, and possibly death. Private citizens spoke in guarded tones, but some congressmen screwed up their courage and accused Huerta of the crime.

Once again the general showed his hand. He issued a decree dissolving Congress. While the legislators were angrily protesting this order, special police broke into the Chamber and arrested 110 congressmen on charges of treason. The prisoners were hauled off to prison in trolley cars amid the jeers and catcalls of a mob of Huerta's hirelings.

When foreign diplomats protested the mass arrests, Huerta said, "Mexico is very sick. I am the doctor and I am forced to prescribe strong medicine or my patient will die."

A local wit's rejoinder to this was, "Yes, Dr. Huerta must prescribe—but does it always have to be castor oil?"

Despite the turmoil and tensions, Huerta confidently predicted that affairs would calm down after the presidential elections scheduled for October 26, 1913. To silence those accusing him of usurping power, Huerta did not enter his name as a candidate for the presidency. But it soon became obvious that this was an empty gesture. Insiders were betting that Huerta would not quit no matter who won the election.

Four candidates were posted: Felix Diaz, Federico

Gamboa, Manuel Calero, and David de la Fuente. Gamboa, serving Huerta as foreign minister, resigned that post to run for president. The election campaign was unique. None of the candidates made a single appearance; none put up a single poster. All four remained in seclusion, afraid to come out in public.

Their apprehensions were well-founded. Each candidate had been privately warned not to campaign, although Huerta made loud assurances of safety to the men. Huerta himself gave the lie to this guarantee. He confided to an American resident of Mexico City, "I wish all the candidates the best of luck. But whoever wins the election won't be alive for his inauguration."

Sunday, October 26, was election day. Before many hours had passed, it became clear that the election was a dismal fiasco. Because it had been a silent campaign without speeches, rallies, posters, or parades, no effort had been made to get out the voters. As a result, hardly any ballots were cast. Some votes were registered, and by no small coincidence they happened to be for Huerta, although he was not listed on the ballot. The voters had taken the trouble to write in his name.

Even before the bogus election was over, one candidate, Felix Diaz, who was hiding out in Veracruz, took sanctuary in the American consulate there, claiming asylum because his life was in danger. That night, he was smuggled out to an American gunboat anchored in Veracruz harbor and from there ferried to the battleship U.S.S. *Louisiana*, which took him to Cuba. The rest of the candidates, following Diaz's lead, also made tracks out of Mexico to havens abroad.

Since the arrest of the 110 congressmen, the Congress had been stacked with army officers who replaced the regular elected legislators. In fact, so many army men held seats in the Chamber that someone suggested that the body should be assembled by blowing a bugle rather than ringing a bell.

Congress was totally under Huerta's rule. He controlled it like a puppet master. Accordingly, Huerta had the legislature declare the election null and void. A new election date was set for July 1914; at the same time, Congress authorized Huerta to carry on as provisional president.

Mexico's Congress never had been much of a legislative body. Under Huerta it became even more of a rubber stamp than it had been during the time of Porfirio Diaz.

After the election farce of October, President Woodrow Wilson definitely decided that the United States would have nothing to do with Huerta. Wilson did everything he could to overthrow the general. He even went to the extent of urging ambassadors of countries that had recognized the Huerta administration to induce the general to retire.

However, retirement was the furthest thing from Huerta's thoughts. He told an American interviewer, "When I retire, I'll be in my coffin!"

Wilson persisted in his efforts to get rid of Huerta. He sent a message to all governments branding Huerta a threat to peace and "the development of Latin America." The American president went even further, saying: "If General Huerta does not retire by force of circumstances, it will become the duty of the United States to use less peaceful means to put him out."

This threat roused indignation in Mexico. In an angry editorial, a Mexico City paper thundered:

> The gringo president claims to believe in democracy. He is a hypocrite of the most shameless sort. What right does he have to interfere in our affairs? The gringo thinks he owns us. He has another think coming. We shall be ruled by men of our choosing—not his!

The Americans did not send another ambassador to Mexico after Henry Lane Wilson left. United States interests were taken care of by the embassy secretary, Nelson O'Shaughnessy, who was given the title chargé d'affaires. But President Wilson wanted his own confidential information on what was happening in Mexico. As his personal agent, he dispatched John Lind, a former governor of Minnesota. A priggish, tight-lipped man of Swedish descent, Lind believed that the main causes of Mexico's troubles were the Catholic church, tequila, and prostitution, in that order.

Just why Woodrow Wilson chose Lind for the delicate mission of sending the White House unbiased and objective reports has remained a mystery. His value as a confidential agent was dubious. Lind was prejudiced and disliked by the Mexicans. He in turn disliked them. From the moment Lind set foot in Mexico, he was under the surveillance of Huerta's secret police. Almost nothing he did could be kept from Huerta.

After the October election, Lind sent several coded messages to President Wilson urging that the United States take positive action against Huerta. He called for open U.S. intervention and a massive sale of arms to the Carranza faction. He warned, "Unless we do something quickly, Mexico will go to pieces. Huerta will not let go until he pulls down the whole house with him."

"I HAVE ROUTED THE ENEMY!"

Huerta's troubles abroad were matched by those at home. The threat of foreign intervention was great. Warships of several countries patrolled the waters around Mexico. Off Veracruz alone, the United States had sixteen ships, the Germans three, the British two, while France and Japan also kept gunboats in the area.

By the end of 1913, the sound financial system Jose Limantour had created for Mexico was in shambles. Each day the peso fell lower on the international money market. A run on banks in Mexico City to exchange pesos for gold and silver created such confusion that Huerta ordered the banks closed for three weeks. The closure was supposed to stabilize the financial situation; instead, the crisis deepened. Huerta was in an economic mess—one that he could not solve by decrees.

The monetary dilemma was only one of many problems. Huerta still had to cope with full-scale revolution. The Constitutionalists were gaining strength each day and Huerta had to bolster his army.

"I need cannon fodder," he said. "And I'll get it!" He resorted to a crude technique for recruiting troops—mass conscription. Quotas were set for each district and they had to be filled. Provost marshals responsible for bringing in the required number of men used any means to get them. Seven hundred spectators at a Mexico City bullfight were seized and marched off to barracks at gunpoint. A crowd at a big fire in the capital was suddenly surrounded by soldiers, and more than a thousand persons, including women, were taken away. Physically fit men went into the army. Those unable to pass the low military medical standards were put to work in an ammunition factory, as were the women. Sudden raids on bars, restaurants, and theaters in Mexico City helped swell the army's ranks. However, these conscripts made poor soldiers.

Meanwhile, up north, the fires of revolution burned. Pancho Villa, resting on his laurels after taking Torreon, decided on a more ambitious project. He determined to take Chihuahua city, the state capital.

Villa knew that by remaining in Torreon he was endangering the Division of the North. Sooner or later, Huerta would send strong forces to recapture the city; the government could not afford the loss of prestige it was suffering by letting Villa hold the communications hub. Also, Villa realized that his troops in Torreon could be outflanked by the enemy. For these reasons and also because his men were getting restless, Villa swung north with his main force, leaving a brigade behind to defend Torreon. His soldiers and camp followers clambered aboard trains and rolled out toward Chihuahua city.

Coaches and freight cars were laden with supplies and people. The cars were so crowded that some people rode inside, some on the roof. A few of the more daring slung hammocks between the car wheels and traveled that way. Every inch of space was occupied. Women rode on the front platforms of locomotives, baking tortillas on the boiler coals. This undisciplined mass wasted ammunition by shooting from the moving trains at cattle, burros, coyotes—anything and everything that moved within sight of the railroad line.

The Division of the North reached Chihuahua city on November 5, 1913. The state capital was defended by seven thousand soldiers and Colorados under a roly-poly fat general named Salvador Mercado. That same day Villa attacked, throwing in his entire division, convinced that his force was strong enough to take the city.

For once, Villa was wrong. The federals not only held, but also mauled the division with accurate artillery fire. After fighting a battle that lasted through the night of November 7, Villa retreated. As the withdrawal began, a shell struck his command post only minutes after he had left. Everyone in the tent was killed.

Though beaten at Chihuahua city, Villa was not discouraged. Another plan came to his mind. Detaching two thousand men from the division, he set off on a risky operation only a week after the battle of Chihuahua city. He was going to use this task force to capture Ciudad Juarez, the border town, about two hundred miles to the north.

Villa hit on a clever stratagem. He captured a southbound federal supply train heading for Chihuahua city and forced the telegrapher at a way station to wire Ciudad Juarez in military code: "Line to Chihuahua city burned by rebels. Cannot proceed. Send orders." Soon, a message from Ciudad Juarez ordered the train to return there.

Villa's men piled on the freight cars and raced through the night for Ciudad Juarez, which the train reached after midnight. The cars lumbered by the sleeping town to a siding in the freight yard. Villa and his soldiers alighted and spread out through the streets, capturing the police station, the barracks, and other strategic centers without firing a shot.

Commanding the Ciudad Juarez garrison were Generals Cesareo Castro and Trucy Aubert, who were captured by Villistas while at a concert. By daybreak, November 15, the most important border town in Mexico had been taken without the loss of a man. Huerta was so upset over the loss of Ciudad Juarez that he accused General Castro of selling out to Villa for $50,000.

Because General Castro had befriended him in the

past, Villa allowed him to cross into Texas. But that was the only mercy Villa showed. He ordered the execution of seventy-four city officials and army officers.

Huerta was committed to recapture Ciudad Juarez and sent a large force to do so. On November 20, as the Division of the North was celebrating the third anniversary of the Madero Revolution, scouts came in with word that a federal force, carried in eleven trains, was on the way to Ciudad Juarez.

Villa sent his cold-blooded aide Fierro to blow up the rail line and delay the enemy as long as possible. Fierro did his job well, destroying the tracks thirty-five miles south of Ciudad Juarez, near a town called Tierra Blanca, where Villa could occupy high ground and hold the federals on a sandy plain with no water supply.

On the afternoon of November 21, about fifty-five hundred federals reached Tierra Blanca and the battle was joined. It continued sporadically until November 25, when Villa launched what he called *un golpe terrifico*— a terrific blow. The golpe was a massed cavalry charge that swept down on federal infantry forming for an attack on the heights.

Caught in the open, the white-uniformed Federalistas broke under the onslaught, fled back to their trains, and retreated to Chihuahua city. Fierro managed to ambush the last train and all aboard were massacred. Villa proudly reported to Carranza, "I have routed the enemy! He is in full and shameless flight!"

In three days of fighting, Huerta had lost a thousand men and the state of Chihuahua. After the debacle at Tierra Blanca, General Mercado no longer could hold Chihuahua city. He abandoned the state capital and in a grueling march reached the border town of Ojinaga. Behind Mercado was the Rio Grande and the safety of the United States only a hundred yards or so away.

Mercado dug in for a last-ditch stand against the pursuing Villistas. Among his thirty-five hundred men, the fat general had forty-five majors, twenty-one colonels, and eleven generals. Mercado's force waited in rifle pits for the enemy, wondering how quickly they could flee across the Rio Grande, when the Villistas showed up.

- 21 -

"IT BEATS OLD AGE!"

After capturing Chihuahua city, Villa rested the Division of the North and prepared for another offensive southward in the direction of Mexico City. He now had sufficient funds to reequip his troops. The banks in Chihuahua city happened to have large sums of gold and silver on hand when he captured the city.

He bought thousands of outmoded U.S. Army khaki uniforms and broad-brimmed campaign hats that once had been issue for American soldiers. Canvas leggings, ammunition belts, Springfield rifles, Colt pistols, hand grenades, sabers, shoes—every military necessity was purchased in quantities. Dealers in such goods flocked to Chihuahua city and wrote up record orders. Seldom if ever before had any Mexican military force been as well turned out as was the Division of the North.

Villa bought up all kinds of job lots wherever they were available. One of his brigades sported magenta socks; another had bright silk bandannas; a third, orchid-colored shirts. Cavalrymen wore automobile goggles because Villa was able to buy them wholesale in gross lots.

Despite the flood of new clothing, most soldiers in the division retained their ragged appearance. Some were clad in overalls, others wore denim or white peasant garb. Footwear ranged from rope sandals to fine cavalry boots. However, every man had a good rifle, a sombrero, a serape, and a bandolier of cartridges.

"Wars are fought with bullets, not uniforms," Villa said. "My boys don't dress well, but they sure can fight when the time comes."

Villa did not always mean everything he said. To contradict himself, he now formed an elite force, splendidly uniformed in fine twill cavalry breeches, olive drab shirts, and expensive wide-brimmed stetson campaign hats.

Known as the *Dorados*—golden ones—for the gold insignia they wore on blouse sleeves and hat crowns, these men, superbly mounted and armed, were organized into three squadrons of one hundred horsemen each. They were recruited from the best horsemen in the division. Every Dorado was issued two horses, two pistols, a carbine, and a saber. They were to be used on special missions and raids.

While Villa was reorganizing, preparations were made to wipe out the last federal pocket in Chihuahua state—General Mercado's troops dug in at Ojinaga. On January 14, 1914, a bitterly cold day, Villa moved against that town. The freezing weather did not keep residents of Presidio, Texas, from clambering to their rooftops to watch the battle just across the river.

The spectators did not see much. Villa sent his Dorados in a golpe terrifico and the defenders broke, stumbling across the Rio Grande in a confused and frightened mass. Camp followers, wailing babies, and soldiers intermingled in the panic-stricken mob. The Villistas took the town in something less than an hour. Villa should have been pleased, but he was furious that General Mercado escaped to safety in the United States along with Pascual Orozco and General Ynes Salazar, a trio that Pancho wanted very much to get his hands on.

The refugees were well treated by the U.S. Army, which set aside more than sixty acres at Fort Bliss for them. The Huertistas were so comfortably fed and housed that a national magazine ran an article decrying the luxuries provided for the internees. The heading of the story read: "If You Get Tired of the Revolution, Come to Fort Bliss for a Rest Cure! Uncle Sam Foots the Bills!"

General Huerta was embarrassed by the loss of Ojinaga and vowed he would have General Mercado shot if he ever came back from internment in the United States. This was not the only setback Huerta suffered. On February 3, 1914, President Woodrow Wilson announced that the United States was lifting its arms embargo on Mexico and would ship weapons to the Constitutionalists, but not Huerta. Since gunrunning from the United States had been going on at a good clip anyway, Wilson's support of Carranza had less impact than it seemed to have. It simply legalized a previously illegal traffic. Although Wilson's action damaged Huerta politically, the general's supporters rallied around him more closely than ever. Government newspapers railed at President Wilson. One declared: "The gringo president is unmasked at last as a friend of bandits and outlaws." When American Chargé d'affaires O'Shaughnessy protested this statement, its author threatened to shoot him.

Wilson's decision to arm Carranza had some unexpected side effects. It was becoming apparent, by February 1914, that France, Great Britain, and Germany were drifting toward war. The Germans, casting about for friends, had begun taking a more active interest in Mexico. Paul von Hintze, the German ambassador to Mexico, sympathized with Huerta, saying that Wilson's move was just another step toward United States occupation of all the territory between Texas and Panama. He made a proposal to Huerta. Germany would give him arms and ammunition if Mexico promised to cut off all oil to England in case of a European war.

Since British support of Huerta was waning, the general accepted the German offer. To show Germany's good faith, the Kaiser's government dispatched to Veracruz from Hamburg three merchant ships laden with munitions and war supplies. The ships, the *Ypiranga*, *Bavaria,* and *Kronprinzessin Cecilie,* were only the first of many ships scheduled to sail from Germany to keep Huerta supplied with weapons and bolster German influence in Mexico.

The Constitutionalists, who had been buttressed by Wilson, received a setback on the very day the arms embargo was lifted. Maximo Castillo, a rebel leader serving with Villa, ambushed a passenger train in the Cumbre Tunnel near Pearson, a town of northern Chihuahua. Castillo was a notorious train robber, and this act had nothing to do with the Revolution. It was for his own profit that he stopped the train. During the course of the holdup, fifty-one passengers, including six Americans, were killed.

Wilson was outraged by this wanton act. So was Pancho Villa. No sooner did he hear of the robbery and the killings than he sent off a column of Dorados to catch Castillo. However, the bandit got away, although seven of his men were captured and shot on the spot.

Castillo made it across the border but was nabbed by U.S. marshals near Huachita, New Mexico, and brought to Fort Bliss for trial. Villa pleaded with American authorities to let him have Castillo. "I'll give him a fair hearing," Villa promised. "He can have a lawyer, a judge, and a jury. Then I'll shoot him." But before the Americans could make up their minds, the bandit-killer solved the problem by dying of advanced tuberculosis in the Fort Bliss jail on May 4, 1914.

The Constitutionalists had received more bad publicity when one of Villa's aides, Rodolfo Fierro, the vicious killer, murdered a man named William Benton, a well-known rancher who had large holdings in northern Chihuahua. Benton had come to Villa's camp to complain about depredations by Villistas on his cattle and property. An argument ensued, and at Villa's bidding Fierro killed Benton.

The death of the rancher brought on international repercussions. The man was a British subject and London protested his violent death, putting the blame on the Americans for arming and encouraging Villa. For a time it appeared that London might openly intervene in Mexico, a step the United States would have had to oppose under the Monroe Doctrine, which declared American responsibility for the tranquillity of the western hemisphere.

The crisis over the Benton slaying was finally obscured by the deepening war clouds over Europe in the spring of 1914. But, for a while, it appeared as though Villa and his murderous sidekick Fierro had touched off the sparks that would bring on a major confrontation between the United States and Great Britain.

Despite the embarrassment created by Castillo and the Benton case, the Americans still backed Carranza and his cause. But the notoriety Villa had gained from the incidents stirred such anxiety in Washington that Wilson decided an effort must be made to persuade Pancho to modify his behavior.

The man chosen to carry out this delicate mission was General Hugh Scott, a veteran army officer who not only spoke fluent Spanish, but also knew the Mexican border from his days of fighting Apaches and Comanches. A clandestine meeting between Scott and Villa was arranged. They came together one midnight in the center of the International Bridge that spanned the Rio Grande between Ciudad Juarez and El Paso.

"I told Villa that civilized people regarded him as a

wild animal." Scott reported. "He expressed surprise and wanted to know why they held such an opinion of him. I cited the killing of Benton and the mass executions of prisoners. I told him I thought he was harming his cause by doing such things."

Villa seemed impressed and confessed to Scott that he really was not cold-blooded. "I don't like to kill anyone. But in the heat of battle I sometimes forget myself. You know how it is. You're a soldier," Villa said.

Scott then handed Villa a pamphlet issued by the U.S. Army on the treatment of prisoners of war and civilians in occupied territories. Villa was so taken with it that he had the pamphlet translated into Spanish and distributed to all his officers.

At a later date he told Scott, "I don't know how much good that will do. Most of my officers can't read. And, as a matter of fact, neither can I. But I've had the booklet read to me and I've had it read to my officers. We'll try to do as it says and follow the rules."

Apparently the army manual did have some beneficial results. The next four hundred prisoners who fell into Villa's clutch were not executed. Instead, he turned them loose in the desert without shoes, food, or water. When Scott pointed out that this was the same as shooting them, Villa replied, "You are wrong, Senor General. If they die, the desert, the heat, and thirst are their killers—not Pancho Villa!"

However, Villa reserved the right to liquidate certain prisoners by firing squads. Captured Colorados were shown no mercy nor allowed even the slim chance of survival they might find in the desert. "I shoot them because they are wicked men," Villa explained. "The Colorados are peons, just like my insurrectos. Any man who turns against his own kind is evil and deserves the extreme penalty!"

Villa also continued to execute captured federal officers. His explanation: "They must be shot because they are educated and should know better than to fight against the Mexican people."

On several occasions, Brigadier General John J. Pershing, commanding United States troops on the border, invited leading rebel commanders, including Alvaro Obregon and Pancho Villa, to the American side of the Rio Grande. Through tact and displays of American military strength, Pershing hoped to show the rebels that the United States had at hand the means to protect American lives and property—by force if necessary.

Pershing liked Obregon and thought him a "sincere and able patriot." However, he was less taken by Villa, whom he regarded as a "different type of man . . . taciturn and restless, shifty-eyed and suspicious."

Timothy Turner, an American journalist, believed that Villa was a shy person, uncomfortable in the presence of those he regarded as his "betters." Pershing once staged a parade at Fort Bliss to which both Villa and Fierro were invited. Turner noted that Villa was overwhelmed by the precision drill of U.S. cavalry units and light artillery batteries. "Like an overgrown child at a circus, he could not conceal his delight, and applauded vigorously when the demonstrations ended. . . . After the review he was made extremely uncomfortable when Pershing invited him to tea at the post commander's headquarters. . . . Fierro was so overcome that he forgot to remove his hat as he entered the house and Villa whispered to him hoarsely, 'Take off your hat, you brute, you animal.' "

Although most observers felt that Obregon, not Villa, was destined to hold high position in the future, Pancho captured the headlines and received all the publicity.

Seventy-one-year-old Ambrose Bierce, one of the best-known American journalists at the time, had been so intrigued by Villa that he had joined the Division of the North to cover the Chihuahua campaign. During the battle of Ojinaga in January 1914, Bierce disappeared and never was seen again. He left behind a note to a relative that provided some hint, but no solution, as to what had happened to him. In his note Bierce said: "If you hear of my being stood up against a Mexican stone wall and shot to rags, please know that it is a pretty good way to depart this life. It beats old age, disease, or falling down the cellar stairs."

- 22 -

"THIS IS A HELL
OF A LITTLE THING"

Early in March 1914, Pancho Villa was back in Chihuahua city, working hard to ready the Division of the North for a drive through the center of the country and then on to Mexico City. Alvaro Obregon was preparing for a push down the difficult terrain of the Pacific coast and, in the northeast, Pablo Gonzalez's oft beaten forces deployed to threaten the oil-rich Gulf coast. As spring came to Mexico, the Constitutionalists were on the march.

However, keeping three armies properly supplied was costly, and Carranza's treasury showed signs of depletion. When Villa requested five million pesos to purchase needed matériel, the First Chief informed him that the money was not to be forthcoming. Villa asked again, and again was told that he could have only one million pesos.

141

Pancho Villa was an elemental soul. When he wanted something enough, he found ways of getting it. In the past, he would have ridden out and stolen the money from bankers or hacendados. But after his talks with General Scott and his visits with General Pershing, Villa felt that he had risen above the ways of banditry. He hit on what he considered a respectable way to get the money.

"If the First Chief won't supply me with funds," Villa announced, "I'll print my own currency."

No sooner said than done. Printing presses were set up in the basement of the governor's palace in Chihuahua city. Printers, engravers, and etchers were found, and before long the presses were merrily clacking away turning out authentic-looking paper pesos.

Villa's money was printed on the best stock and elegantly decorated with fine scrollwork. The bills bore indecipherable but impressively scrawled signatures and had pictures of Villa's two martyred heroes, Francisco Madero and Abraham Gonzalez. Because of the two portraits, the bills were known as *dos caras,* or two faces.

Of course, Villista currency was not secured either by gold or silver, so it was said that the dos caras had the same value as a two-faced friend—not very much. The flood of paper pesos from Villa's presses worried Carranza, who sent a financial expert to explain to Villa why he must stop printing money.

Pancho listened to the financial man's explanation for a few minutes and then interrupted him. "I don't give a damn what you say," Villa roared. "I need money and if the First Chief doesn't give it to me, I'll print my own, understand? Now go back and tell Carranza this!"

The expert scooted away and reported to Carranza. A day or so later Villa was informed that he could have all the legal money he needed if only he would stop the flow of dos caras. Villa readily agreed. He told an American journalist: "I knew I'd shake up the old man. Those big fellows don't really care about the Revolution. They

142

do care about money and that's how to get at them!"

Villa made still another request of the First Chief. General Felipe Angeles was in Carranza's cabinet as minister of war and Villa wanted him to be artillery commander for the Division of the North. Angeles, who had been freed by Huerta after Madero's death, had joined Carranza when the rebellion began. After Villa's request, this cultured, Paris-educated soldier was detached for service with the rebel leader and led a crack artillery corps made up of revolutionary regular army officers and men. Though he was Villa's superior intellectually and militarily, the general faithfully and loyally served the untutored peasant.

Because he had long admired Villa, Angeles held a ceremony in Pancho's honor at the governor's palace in Chihuahua city. A special medal to be presented Villa was struck for the occasion. Since Villa hated public appearances, he was not told about the affair until the last moment. He showed up at the governor's palace in a crumpled khaki uniform that had several buttons missing. His hair was uncombed and he needed a shave.

Inside the courtyard, the officers of the artillery corps were resplendent in blue dress uniforms. A company of soldiers stood at present arms as Villa entered. He was escorted to a velvet-covered chair on a dais and there he slouched, listening to six speeches extolling his heroism in combat.

Then a band played a lively march. An elegantly clad officer presented Villa with a small box that contained the medal Angeles had designed for him. Villa held it up for all to see. He grinned at the audience and in a loud voice said, "This is a hell of a little thing to give a man for all that heroism you're talking about." Then he let fly a stream of tobacco juice and shambled off between the files of saluting troops.

The Division of the North went into action again shortly after the ceremony. This time the objective was

Torreon, which Villa had captured six months earlier; it had been retaken by Huerta and now the Constitutionalists were out to seize it for good. The campaign was eminently successful. Villa not only took Torreon and a huge store of war supplies, but pushed on to San Pedro de las Colonias, forty-five miles northeast of the captured town. San Pedro also fell to Villa and hundreds of federal soldiers deserted to his side, while others abandoned their weapons and uniforms, donned civilian clothes, and went home.

The war in Chihuahua was almost over; the road to Mexico City lay practically open. Villa would have pressed on to the capital, but his troops were too exhausted for such a strenuous drive. He needed reinforcements, fresh horses, and additional equipment before pushing on to Mexico City.

While Villa halted to refit, Obregon moved on the Pacific coast. He took one town after another and laid siege to the strongly held port of Mazatlan. Even Pablo Gonzalez, Carranza's least competent general, swung into action that spring. He handled his troops well for a change. Faking an attack on Monterrey and Saltillo, he moved his main force down the coast to the important oil port of Tampico. This was a vital objective. The rebels needed a Gulf port and wanted oil-rich Tampico, where foreign-owned wells pumped many barrels of oil daily for shipment to United States refineries.

Carranza was eager to share in the oil trade profits and urged Gonzalez to speed up his offensive against Tampico. By the end of March, Gonzalez was poised some ten miles from the city, and on April 5 the long-awaited attack got under way. It was destined to have far greater repercussions than either Carranza or Huerta could have foreseen.

"IS IT A CALAMITY?"

Just prior to the opening of the assault on Tampico, John Lind, the half-forgotten personal envoy of President Wilson, briefly emerged from the obscurity into which he had slipped. Lind's clumsy snooping and probing had made him a comic figure to the Mexicans. Back in Washington, the State Department and the White House were growing tired of his cables filled with impractical suggestions and petty complaints.

Toward the end of March, Lind came up with what he considered to be a brilliant solution to the Huerta problem. In a long, encoded cable to the White House, he outlined a plan for the capture of Mexico City and Huerta's overthrow. Lind revealed that he had summoned to Mexico City a Spanish-speaking U.S. marine officer in disguise. The leatherneck had drawn detailed maps of the city's defenses after scouting them out. A raiding party had been formed to slip into Mexico City and, in some vague way, take possession of it.

Huerta was to be captured and held until turned over to the proper authorities, who would deal with him "according to law." Lind requested permission from Washington to go ahead with his outlandish scheme. The only answer he received was that the president "did not contemplate any immediate action."

Crushed by this curt rebuff, Lind cabled his resignation to President Wilson and sailed for the United States on the first available ship from Veracruz. He left

Mexico on April 6, in time to miss all the action he had been espousing for so many months.

Because the Americans had vast oil interests along the Gulf coast of Mexico, the Navy kept an unusually large squadron in the area. The Fourth Division of the Atlantic Fleet, Rear Admiral Frank Friday Fletcher commanding, was at Veracruz. The Fifth Division, under Rear Admiral Henry T. Mayo, held the Tampico station. At that port also were the British cruiser H.M.S. *Hermione* and the German cruiser *Dresden*, on patrol to safeguard the interests of their nationals.

Since the port of Tampico was located about ten miles up the shallow Panuco River, Admiral Mayo made his headquarters aboard the U.S.S. *Dolphin*, a gunboat that could negotiate the Panuco, and not the U.S.S. *Minnesota* or the U.S.S. *Connecticut*, the battleships of the Fifth Division. Rarely in United States naval history had a rear admiral's burgee flown from the masthead of a ship as lowly as the *Dolphin*.

By April 7, rebel forces had reached a bridge that spanned a canal marking Tampico's northern boundary. When fighting broke out along the canal line, the numerous oil installations in the area had to shut down.

Under orders from Admiral Mayo, the *Dolphin* was cooperating with Clarence Miller, the United States consul in Tampico, in the evacuation of American oil workers and their families from the combat zone. The *Dolphin* would put in at Tampico port, take on a load of passengers, and ferry them out to larger warships anchored at the mouth of the Panuco.

On April 7, much to the chagrin of the squadron supply officer, it was discovered that the *Dolphin* and other dispatch boats were running short of oil. This created an embarrassing situation for the U.S. Navy, situated as it was in the midst of one of the world's richest oil fields. Since the fighting had caused all American-owned installations to close, locating a source of oil for the *Dolphin* presented a problem.

The gunboat's skipper, Lieutenant Commander Ralph K. Earle, went ashore and learned that Max Tyron, a German oil dealer, had large quantities of refined oil stored in a warehouse on the canal in the heart of the war zone. Despite her shallow draft, the *Dolphin* could not negotiate these waters, so Earle sent an ensign named Charles Copp and a detail in a whaleboat to Tyron's warehouse. Disregarding bullets zipping overhead, the American work party sailed serenely up the canal to the warehouse, convinced that the large American flags they flew fore and aft would provide a safeguard.

Copp and his men were loading cans of fuel onto the whaleboat when a detachment of federal troops came on the double and placed the Americans under arrest. The officer in charge told Copp he had orders to keep that area clear of all noncombatants and neutrals. The unarmed Americans were marched through the town to the headquarters of Colonel Ramon Hinojosa, the sector commander. The colonel lectured Ensign Copp on the folly of entering a combat zone, but then let the whaleboat's crew go back to the warehouse to complete loading the fuel. Once that was done the whaleboat returned to the *Dolphin*.

Almost as soon as the whaleboat arrived, a messenger came to the American vessel with a letter from General Ignacio Morelos Zaragoza, the commandant in Tampico. Morelos Zaragoza apologized profusely to Commander Earle and to U.S. Consul Miller for the brief detention of Copp and his men.

Earle and Miller were satisfied and made a routine report of the incident to Admiral Mayo, fully believing that the case was closed. However, Mayo was a cantankerous man noted for a nasty temper and a petty habit of holding grudges. To everyone's surprise, he rejected the Mexican apology. He sent an officer with a note to Morelos Zaragoza demanding a formal public apology, the punishment of the officer who had arrested the whaleboat crew, and the promise that the general would hoist the American flag "in a prominent position on the shore and render it a twenty-one-gun salute."

Mayo was acting on his own. He neither asked for nor received instructions from Washington and did not even consult with Admiral Fletcher. Meanwhile, General Morelos Zaragoza, alarmed by the new twist, advised Mayo that he would have to await word from Mexico City before doing anything further. This minor incident was being blown up out of all proportion to its significance.

That same day, Mayo finally told Fletcher what had happened and the latter backed him fully. The admirals sent off a joint report to Washington about the Tampico incident. On April 10, President Wilson, through Secretary of State William Jennings Bryan, advised Chargé d'affaires O'Shaughnessy in Mexico City to "handle the matter with the utmost earnestness, firmness, and frankness, representing to the Mexicans its extreme seriousness."

An improbable touch was introduced when O'Shaughnessy met with Roberto Esteva Ruiz, the Mexican government's undersecretary for foreign relations. Esteva Ruiz suggested that O'Shaughnessy have a talk with President Huerta, but the general was nowhere to be found until tracked down at one of his drinking haunts. Huerta, befuddled with brandy, had to be introduced by O'Shaughnessy to Esteva Ruiz. The president claimed he never even had heard of his own undersecretary and certainly had never met him.

Huerta mulled over the Tampico matter for a couple of days, and on April 12 issued a formal response to Mayo. He stated flatly that General Morelos Zaragoza's written apology to Earle and Miller was sufficient and refused Mayo's demand for a salute to the American flag. The arresting officer and Colonel Hinojosa had been reprimanded—punishment enough under the circumstances, Huerta thought.

Stirred to righteous indignation, the Americans were not willing to call it quits. John Lind arrived in Washington on April 13 and was summoned by Wilson for advice. Lind was clever enough to tell the president precisely what he wanted to hear—be firm with Huerta. Indeed, Lind slyly suggested, this might be the very chance Wilson had been seeking to bring about the ouster of Huerta.

The following day—April 14—Wilson called a meeting of his cabinet, which agreed unanimously that the American flag must be saluted. Late that afternoon, Wilson ordered the whole Atlantic Fleet to Tampico—a mighty concentration of warships ranging from battle-wagons to gunboats.

When Huerta learned what was going on, he said, "Is it a calamity? I don't think so. It's the best thing that could take place for us." He explained his belief that the Mexican people would unite against this Yankee aggression and save his tottering government. Because he felt this way, Huerta stood firm and told O'Shaughnessy he would not change his mind and yield to American insistence on saluting the Stars and Stripes.

Then two other incidents, wholly unrelated, heated up the crisis between the United States and Mexico. Like the Tampico affair, they had a lopsided impact and were exaggerated by President Wilson. In Veracruz, an American naval mail clerk was arrested at the post office by a Mexican soldier who mistakenly thought the man was a deserter wanted by U.S. authorities. A reward had been posted for the fugitive and the Mexican soldier believed he was going to collect it. The whole thing was quickly smoothed over; the sailor was released, the soldier disciplined.

This time, Admiral Fletcher reported to Washington that the Mexican authorities had acted "impeccably" and that there was no cause for complaint against them. "The incident has no import whatsoever," Fletcher concluded.

The same day a diplomatic message from Washington was held up nearly an hour by the Mexico City censor's office. According to O'Shaughnessy, this was done without malice, but only through a misunderstanding of his duties by a newly appointed censor. "There was no intent to harass or impede communications between Washington and Mexico City," stated O'Shaughnessy in his official report.

If it had been left to O'Shaughnessy and Fletcher, both trifling cases would have been forgotten. But President Wilson needed more fuel for the fire he was kindling, and he used these minor events to stoke the flames. He called to his office the members of the Senate Foreign Relations Committee and outlined to them the measures he was proposing to take.

"For some time," he said, "this country has been suffering intolerable insults in Mexico . . . the Mexican government has seemed to think mere apologies sufficient when the rights of American citizens or the dignity of the United States is involved." He then told the senators that he intended to seize Tampico and Veracruz "to show the Mexicans that they cannot, with impunity, insult our flag."

The committee gave Wilson solid support. Cried one senator, "I'd make 'em salute the flag if we had to blow up the whole place!"

Huerta was given a last chance. O'Shaughnessy was instructed to see him again and persuade him to order a twenty-one-gun salute to the American flag. Huerta refused, stating that it was an "unnecessary humiliation for my country."

Seeing the futility of further attempts at persuading Huerta, O'Shaughnessy cabled Washington on April 18, "I regret most profoundly my failure to bring Huerta to reason."

When his message arrived in Washington, President Wilson was at the Washington Country Club for his customary round of Saturday golf. When a courier brought him the final word from Mexico City, the president was teeing off on the fourteenth green. Wilson hurried from the golf course to his office. The White House corridor was jammed with newsmen waiting to find out what he would do.

On his own typewriter, the president tapped out an ultimatum and had it distributed to the reporters. He warned that unless the Mexicans agreed to comply with Admiral Mayo's demands within twenty-four hours, he intended to place the issue before Congress "with a view of taking such action as may be necessary to enforce respect due to the nation's flag."

- 24 -

"I HAVE NO ENTHUSIASM FOR WAR"

President Wilson passed Sunday, April 19, with his ailing wife, Ellen, who was under treatment at a sanatorium in White Sulphur Springs, West Virginia. The day went by without word from Huerta, but Wilson bided his time. Early Monday morning, he returned to Washington and called a cabinet meeting. He outlined a speech he intended for Congress that afternoon and then revealed news of a disturbing nature that had come from the

United States consul at Veracruz. The German ship *Ypiranga* was steaming toward that port with a cargo of two hundred machine guns and fifteen million rounds of ammunition for Huerta.

According to Wilson's thinking, an arms shipment of that size must not be allowed to land because it strengthened Huerta. The president never did explain why a neutral nation should be so concerned or involved in Mexico's domestic affairs.

Because of this development, Admiral Mayo, who was making ready for a move against Tampico, was ordered to reinforce Fletcher at Veracruz. The rest of the Atlantic Fleet, slowly heading for Tampico, was ordered by wireless to make for Veracruz at flank speed.

Before delivering his speech to Congress, Wilson held a press conference at which he said: "In no conceivable circumstances would we fight the people of Mexico. It is only an issue between this government and a person calling himself the provisional president of Mexico whose right to call himself such we never have recognized in any way. . . . I have no enthusiasm for war; but I have enthusiasm for the dignity of the United States."

As the president finished, a reporter called out, "Mr. President, are you saying that we're going to wage war on an individual—Senor Huerta?"

Wilson made no reply and walked haughtily from the room. A little later he spoke to a joint session of Congress, stressing that American honor must be restored through armed action against Huerta. When he finished, the members of both houses gave him a standing ovation and voted approval of his decision to act in Mexico.

William Canada, the United States consul in Veracruz, telephoned the White House at 2:00 A.M., April 21, that the *Ypiranga* was going to dock later that morning. Three freight trains were waiting at dockside to rush the guns and ammunition to Mexico City. Now the time had come for the president to make his moves. A few minutes after talking to Canada, Wilson arranged a three-way telephone conversation with Secretary of State Bryan and Secretary of the Navy Josephus Daniels. Their discussion became known as the "Pajama Conference" because of the attire the participants were wearing.

After some exchanges, Daniels and Bryan agreed with Wilson that the German munitions must not be allowed to reach Huerta. Wilson then told Daniels to order the Veracruz customshouse seized to prevent the unloading of the *Ypiranga*. Quite pleased with himself, the president went back to bed unrealistically certain that no blood would be spilled when U.S. marines and sailors came ashore to take the customshouse.

At 8:00 A.M., April 21, Rear Admiral Frank Fletcher received his orders from Daniels: "Seize customshouse. Do not permit war supplies delivered to Huerta or any other party." Fletcher was not a man to waste time. Although Mayo and the Atlantic Fleet had not yet arrived, he decided to move at once with the forces at hand. Fletcher advised Consul Canada that American forces would start landing at 11:00 A.M. At that time, Canada was to tell the federal commander, General Gustavo Maass, what was taking place.

Mustering a landing party of eight hundred sailors and marines, Fletcher also sent the battleship U.S.S. *Utah* to intercept the *Ypiranga* and have her drop anchor outside the harbor. The first boatloads of sailors and marines headed for shore precisely at 11:00 A.M. Watching them through field glasses, Consul Canada telephoned Maass as he had been instructed to do.

The general was shocked. Despite Canada's assurances that the landing force would not proceed beyond the customshouse, he ordered his men to repel the invaders. But the federal troops put up only token resistance. Most of the units Maass ordinarily commanded had been sent to hold the line at Tampico. Gaps in the ranks were filled by convicts released from the fortress prison San Juan de Ulua. They were a poor substitute for frontline troops.

By 11:30 A.M. the American marines and sailors had landed. A large crowd gathered at the dock to watch them debark from the whaleboats. At first, the Mexicans were good-natured and friendly, but when they realized what was going on their attitude changed to hostility.

The customshouse was occupied quickly, but American zeal soon superseded orders. The landing party took over the railway depot, post office, and telegraph office, too. They set up roadblocks and sited machine guns at strategic points. It was a finely handled maneuver, an exercise in seizing and occupying a city. The landing looked more like a seaborne invasion than a mere police action.

Maass got word from Mexico City not to fight the Americans but to pull back to Tejeria, a town about ten miles inland. He complied, but could not control all his men. Small federal units independently battled the hated gringos. While a great many shots were fired, very few Americans were hit, due to the notoriously poor marksmanship of the Mexicans. By nightfall, Consul Canada reported four men killed and twenty wounded.

The ships of the Fifth Division and the bulk of the Atlantic Fleet arrived during the hours of darkness. At daybreak, Wednesday, April 22, more than three thousand sailors and marines were being ferried ashore to complete the occupation of Veracruz.

The invaders met little organized resistance, but snipers took a steady toll of them. The Americans retaliated with overwhelming firepower. Mexican casualties ran high, and mounted alarmingly when the warships U.S.S. *Prairie,* U.S.S. *Chester,* and U.S.S. *San Francisco* bombarded the naval academy, where a detachment of cadets was putting up sharp resistance. The ships' big guns demolished the academy, killing and wounding a large number of cadets.

Before noon on April 22, except for minor mopping-up operations, the city of Veracruz was firmly in American hands. The landing force had suffered nineteen killed and seventy wounded. Mexican losses ran into the hundreds. Among them were a few soldiers, many snipers or civilians suspected of being snipers, and innocent men, women, and children who had happened to get in the way of shells or bullets. The Americans conducted a house-to-house search in the hunt for snipers, and by evening the city was slowly returning to normal. But the gutted buildings, bullet-riddled walls, shattered glass, debris in the streets, and American patrols showed that this was not a normal time.

Reaction to the American aggression at Veracruz was swift in coming. Huerta declared, "Fellow Mexicans! We shall defend ourselves with honor. The Republic of Mexico has been, is, and always will be in the right. The government serenely and confidently awaits the turn of events."

This was a mild statement from Huerta, but the press was not so restrained. A Mexico City newspaper shrieked, "We May Die, But Let Us Kill!" Other papers clamored for unity in the face of the American threat. For a time, this seemed to be a possibility.

From his Chihuahua city headquarters, Venustiano Carranza, bursting with patriotism, proclaimed: "The invasion of our country may bring us to war with our powerful neighbor to the north. . . . I call upon the American government to cease its hostile acts against us and order its forces from our country before it is too late."

Alvaro Obregon wanted to fight the Americans, and called upon his troops to prepare for a battle against the "Yankee imperialists." But Pancho Villa saw things in a different light. "It's Huerta's bull that's being gored," he said. "For my part, the Americans can keep Veracruz so tight that not even water from the harbor could get in to Huerta. . . . No drunkard like him can draw me into a war against my friends, the Americans!"

The American occupation of Veracruz was good for the Constitutionalists. While Carranza and others protested on patriotic grounds, Villa was analyzing the situation from a revolutionary's point of view. Veracruz was the chief port through which supplies were funneled to Huerta, who would soon be strangled by the loss of this port. Villa was completely satisfied when American officers reassured him that the invasion would not go a mile farther inland. Possibly Carranza also understood the advantages of having the Americans in control of Veracruz, but spoke as he did for the benefit of his public image.

The Veracruz operation evoked violent anti-American outbursts in Mexico City. The statue of George Washington that had been presented in September 1910 was pulled down and smashed by an enraged mob. American flags were spat upon, burned, tied to the tails of donkeys, used for shining shoes and cleaning streets. Bands of youths chanting, "Death to the gringos!" roamed throughout the capital, smashing, burning, and looting American-owned shops and offices. Few Americans dared venture alone into the streets, and no one went anywhere unarmed. Hysteria swept the border towns of Texas, where residents rushed to buy guns and ammunition as rumors grew of Mexican mobs on the way to massacre everyone on the American side of the Rio Grande.

President Wilson was upset by the fury he had unleashed. In a meaningless gesture, he again placed an embargo on arms for Carranza, declaring that he was taking this step to show America's neutrality in Mexico's domestic affairs. The rebels at once went back to their old practice of smuggling in all the guns and ammunition they needed.

156

As the tense situation grew daily tenser, the German ship *Ypiranga* slipped away from Veracruz harbor, where she was being watched by the Americans, and sailed to a small Mexican port farther south to unload her cargo of war supplies. She was joined by a second German munitions ship, the *Bavaria,* which was carrying two million rounds of rifle ammunition and eight thousand rolls of barbed wire. The delivery of the munitions made a mockery of the lives lost during the battle of Veracruz.

The threat of war between the United States and Mexico hung oppressively in the air. Wilson, who had never expected matters to go as far as they had, mobilized the U.S. regular army of 54,000 officers and men, and called out the 150,000-strong National Guard.

The danger of a conflict was lessened somewhat when Argentina, Brazil, and Chile offered to mediate the crisis. Numerous meetings were held in which little was accomplished. But while the talks continued there was no war. President Wilson began to adopt a more conciliatory tone toward Mexico, much to the dismay of certain hawkish politicians who wanted to take Mexico City and kick Huerta out.

The occupation force at Veracruz was swelled to seven thousand men with the arrival of the Fifth Brigade under General Frederick Funston, who cabled Secretary of War Lindley Garrison: "Say the word and you'll have Mexico City on a silver platter . . . just give the order and leave the rest to me!"

But the only order Funston received was, "Stay where you are!" Thus, the seven thousand American soldiers, sailors, and marines were left to sweat out a summer in Veracruz's miserable clime while the Mexicans settled their differences with more violence and bloodshed.

- 25 -

"I DRINK TO THE
NEW PRESIDENT OF MEXICO!"

By the end of April 1914, even Huerta's most optimistic supporters had to concede that the tide was running against their man. Bumbling Pablo Gonzalez took Monterrey, the biggest city in the north, on April 24. Tampico came under heavy attack on May 10, and the rebels used the fires of burning oil tanks to light their way in night assaults. Four days later, after both sides had taken heavy losses, the oil center fell to the rebels. Pablo Gonzalez's forces suffered more than fifteen hundred casualties, while General Morelos Zaragoza tallied over half of his five-thousand-man garrison as killed, wounded, missing, or captured.

The last Huertista stronghold in northern Mexico was Saltillo, reinforced by survivors of the Torreon and Monterrey garrisons. Discussion opened among Constitutionalist leaders over who should lead the final offensive against Saltillo. This controversy brought a split between Pancho Villa and Venustiano Carranza, ending that unlikely union.

The disagreement started when Villa, in Torreon, started to make final preparations for an assault on Zacatecas, a weakly defended mining town straddling the road to Mexico City. With Zacatecas in rebel hands, the last obstacle on the road to Mexico City would be eliminated. The Division of the North was in excellent shape for the drive to the national capital. Just as Villa was ready to move out, Carranza showed up in Torreon and ordered Pancho to move against Saltillo because the federals there were endangering the Constitutionalist flank. Villa knew this to be the truth—Saltillo was a threat —but Pablo Gonzalez had large forces only 50 miles from Saltillo, while Villa would have to march more than 180 miles to reach it.

Both Villa and General Felipe Angeles tried to reason with Carranza. They would take Zacatecas first and then take care of Saltillo. But this was the last thing Carranza wished to happen. He knew that when the Division of the North moved in the direction of Mexico City it would never stop until the capital had been taken.

Carranza did not want Villa to be the one to capture Mexico City. The people, overwhelmed by hero worship, might make Villa, not Carranza, their president. This was a condition unthinkable for the First Chief. Stubbornly, he insisted that Villa march on Saltillo. After a long, heated argument, Pancho threw up his hands and cried, "Who can sway this man—our First Chief? Let's do as he asks, Angeles. Let's see if we can please him!"

Reluctantly, Angeles agreed, although it went against his better military judgment. Accordingly, on May 11, the Division of the North turned its collective face toward Saltillo. Six days later, the division was at Paredon, a town bordering the objective. Paredon was defended by five thousand federals. They did not put up much of a fight and fled in disorder when Villa threw eight thousand cavalry troopers into a final, thundering charge.

On May 20, Saltillo was taken without a battle. The Federalistas deserted by the hundreds and Huerta's army simply melted away. Villa remained at Saltillo until the end of the month, when he turned the town over to Pablo Gonzalez, who had arrived belatedly with his division. The two rebel leaders had a cordial meeting and decided that the triumphal entry into Mexico City should be jointly made by Villa, Gonzalez, and Obregon, the three whose men had borne the brunt of the fighting.

Naturally, this arrangement made Carranza unhappy. The First Chief called upon all his political guile to foil the idea of a triumvirate victory march. He went to Durango and met with a minor rebel general, Panfilo Natera, to whom he entrusted the attack against Zacatecas. But Natera lacked both strength and skill for the mission. Although Zacatecas had only a small garrison, Natera was soundly beaten when he attacked early in June. On June 11, he called for reinforcements and Carranza asked Villa to supply them.

From his headquarters in Saltillo, the First Chief ordered Villa, now back in Torreon, to detach five thousand men from the Division of the North and rush them to Natera at Zacatecas. However, Villa wanted to keep his division intact for the drive south, and so advised Carranza by telegraph.

The First Chief repeated his order and Villa reiterated the objections to it. Telegrams flew back and forth—Carranza insisting on having his way, Villa standing firm on his refusal to break up the division. In Saltillo, surrounded by staff officers, Carranza dictated orders to a telegrapher. In Torreon, surrounded by staff officers, Villa shot back increasingly hot replies. At last, Villa's notorious temper flared. In a fit of anger, he wired Carranza: "Senor, I resign command of the division. To whom shall I deliver it?"

This turn pleased Carranza. He had long regarded Villa as a rival, and now that threat seemed to be eliminated. But he would not have been so happy had he been aware of what was going on in Torreon, where Villa's officers boiled in mutinous wrath.

General Maclovio Herrera was so furious that he ordered a telegrapher to send the message: "Senor Carranza, I am informed of your treatment of my General

Francisco Villa. Senor First Chief, you are a dirty dog and a pig!" Herrera had a loaded pistol pointed at the telegrapher's head to make sure he transmitted the wire when General Angeles strode into the telegraph office. Angeles, who had been inspecting outposts, had not participated in the telegraphic confrontation between Carranza and Villa. As a regular army officer, he was a stickler for discipline. He was also a forceful man, and soon convinced Herrera not to have the message sent.

But when Carranza ordered the division's officers to elect a new commander, Angeles was the first to disobey. In the name of all the officers of the division, he wired Carranza a refusal. "We are sticking with Villa," the telegram said. However, Carranza was persistent and Villa's officers had to choose between their general and Carranza. It was an easy decision to make. Again acting as spokesman for the rest, Angeles telegraphed the First Chief: "We do not accept your order. We well know that you were seeking an opportunity to stop Villa . . . because of your purpose to remove from the revolutionary scene the men who can think without your orders, who do not flatter and praise you."

Now the break had come, but it had come too late to help Huerta or to harm the Revolution. Backed by his own officers and men, Villa acted as though nothing had happened between him and Carranza. He merely ignored anything the First Chief said or did.

On June 17, without informing Carranza, Villa moved the entire Division of the North to Zacatecas. By the twentieth, more than twenty-three thousand rebel troops surrounded the town. After two days spent deploying his forces and siting his artillery, Villa attacked at 10:00 A.M., June 23.

The division delivered a tremendous golpe and practically wiped out the garrison, which had numbered over twelve thousand officers and men. It was conservatively estimated that only two hundred Huertistas got away.

The rout was complete, according to Villa. "The enemy fled," he stated, "leaving us their cannon, their machine guns, and almost all their rifles. . . . They also left us their supplies and their munitions."

Pleased by his overwhelming victory, Villa was willing to make up with Carranza and sent him details of the Zacatecas operation as though the break never had taken place. But if Villa was conciliatory, Carranza was not. The First Chief refused to mend the rift with Villa and found a way to hamstring him.

The one item the Division of the North had not captured at Zacatecas was coal to fuel its trains. When Carranza learned this, he shut off all fuel supplies to Villa, leaving him stranded at Zacatecas. Unable to move on Mexico City, Villa fumed and stormed and scoured the countryside for coal. Carranza shunted all reinforcements and supplies to Obregon and Pablo Gonzalez, both of whom now were advancing in a southerly direction and moving toward the national capital.

Carranza turned all his energies toward keeping Villa from Mexico City; the First Chief had learned that once the capital was taken, Villa intended to propose to the top generals that they choose a new leader to replace Carranza.

It soon became apparent that Obregon held the inside track in the race for Mexico City. His Division of the Northwest crossed the Pacific mountains and on July 6 took Mexico's second largest city, Guadalajara. Nothing stood between Obregon and the capital. Placing his trust in Obregon, Carranza urged him to seize Mexico City with "all possible speed."

But speed no longer was of importance. The Huerta regime was collapsing on its own. The day before the fall of Guadalajara, Huerta announced that elections for a new president would be held that very day—July 5. No list of candidates was presented, no one came to vote, and the election existed only in Huerta's alcohol-befuddled brain.

However, he was alert enough to see that the rebels were cutting off his escape routes one by one. If they caught him, the firing squad was a certainty. General Huerta was no coward, but he had a lust for life and was a good enough soldier to know when he had been beaten. It was time to pull out.

He did so, but first he went through the legality of resignation according to the constitution. On July 9, he appointed Francisco Carvajal, the chief justice of the Supreme Court, as his secretary of foreign relations. This put Carvajal in line for the presidency after Huerta and Vice-President General Aureliano Blanquet. Huerta submitted his own resignation to the Chamber of Deputies on July 15 and then retired to the Colon, his favorite drinking place. According to an observer, a crowd followed him every step of the way, cheering and applauding the newly resigned president. Huerta filled his glass, lifted it high, and said to the onlookers, "This will be my last drink here. I drink to the new president of Mexico."

A few days later, July 17, he slipped quietly out of the country, by way of the small port of Puerto Mexico, on the German cruiser *Dresden*.

He was piped formally aboard with full honors. On August 1, 1914, Huerta landed in Spain, and three days later World War I engulfed Europe. When the news of the catastrophe broke, Huerta was drinking brandy in a Barcelona café. With a flash of his old humor, he quipped, "This is one war they can't blame on me!"

PART

IV

The Constitutionalist

"WE MUST TALK OF
MEXICO CITY"

The last Huertista stronghold to fall was San Luis Potosi, 250 miles north of Mexico City. It was taken July 15, by Jesus Carranza, the First Chief's brother. With the capture of San Luis Potosi, hostilities between the Huertistas and the Constitutionalist forces ceased. Carranza's men made ready to converge on Mexico City.

Francisco Carvajal, the man who had taken over from Huerta, appealed to Carranza for a meeting to arrange a peaceful entry into the capital. With customary bullheadedness, Carranza rejected any talks.

"I am interested only in unconditional surrender," he declared. "And while I give my assurances that no excesses will be permitted by my forces, I promise that all who supported Huerta—civilian or military—will be punished as enemies of democracy."

As July came to an end, Carranza took further steps to balk a Villa occupation of the capital. Obregon's troops were moved to a rail center on the route that Villa would have to follow to reach Mexico City. At the same time, Pablo Gonzalez moved his division into a position to support Obregon. The Division of the North could reach Mexico City only if Villa chose to fight the rest of the Constitutionalist army.

Villa seemed in no hurry for such an unpalatable

encounter. He spent his time reinforcing and resupplying his division. Everyone knew this was in preparation for a showdown with Carranza. The United States consul in Chihuahua city notified Washington that another Mexican civil war was highly likely.

The main question was how to occupy Mexico City without bloodshed. Carranza's uncompromising demand for unconditional surrender did not make matters any lighter. Officials in the capital who had worked with Huerta dared not linger; they knew a firing squad was waiting. From President pro tem Carvajal on down, they fled into exile.

The only one who dared remain was Eduardo Iturbide, the governor of the Federal District—a capital area like the District of Columbia, in which Washington is located. To Iturbide fell the difficult mission of keeping order in Mexico City. It was an almost impossible task.

Carranza had demanded that the capital's garrison be withdrawn before Constitutionalist troops entered the city. But Emiliano Zapata's skirmishers were harassing the capital's outlying districts, held up only by federal troops. If these were withdrawn, the chances were that Zapata could take Mexico City before Carranza's men arrived.

At last Carranza conceded that the federal garrison should remain in the capital. This decision angered Zapata, who regarded it as a hostile act by the First Chief. Zapata had opposed Diaz, Madero, and Huerta. The self-styled "Attila of the South" was now prepared to fight Carranza. It was destined to be a war lasting five cruel years. Actually, the fact that both Zapata and Carranza were against Huerta had not made them allies. A quirk of history had placed them both on the same side. There had been little or no communication between Carranza and Zapata from the start to the finish of the struggle against Huerta.

Obregon's division reached Teoloycuan, a hamlet

twenty miles north of Mexico City, on August 9. Two days later, a delegation from the capital headed by Iturbide came to settle the details for the take-over of Mexico City. Iturbide had made out his will before leaving the capital. "I am a fatalist," he said. "What will be, will be. But it is better to be prepared for it."

The district governor spent an uncomfortable time in Obregon's camp. Upon his arrival there, he was told that the chances were that he would be shot before the day was over. "No federal officer or official ever has left my encampment alive," Obregon said.

"I am prepared to die," Iturbide responded. "But first let us talk. What we have to discuss is more important than my life. We must talk of Mexico City and what will have to be done about conditions there."

That night, Carranza arrived in Teoloycuan and negotiations began on August 14. The First Chief refused to take an active part in the talks. He let Obregon do all the bargaining and sign the agreement stating that federal forces would withdraw to Puebla and leave behind all surplus arms and ammunition.

The Mexico City police would be charged with maintaining law and order until the Constitutionalists arrived. All this was conceded by Iturbide after Obregon's promise that the victors would not molest the residents of the capital.

The federals marched out of Mexico City on August 15, but their numbers were depleted by scores of Colorados who had deserted during the night, fleeing to Morelos where most of them joined Zapata. He welcomed the Colorados though he despised them. But Zapata needed men for the coming battles with Carranza and was certain the Colorados would fight desperately, for their lives already were forfeit.

"If they think to betray me, I'll take care of them. We have many stone walls in Morelos," Zapata said, referring to the firing squad.

Obregon's Division of the Northwest marched into Mexico City during the early afternoon of August 15. On hand to greet them was Eduardo Iturbide, who gallantly offered himself as a prisoner of war. Impressed by the man's bravery and integrity, Obregon sent him home.

Three days later, August 18, Carranza made his triumphal entry into the city. The occasion was flawed by the refusal of Pablo Gonzalez to participate because Carranza had given Obregon the post of honor, the right of the line, while Pablo Gonzalez was relegated to the left. That minor dispute was an augury for the future. Carranza was in the capital as provisional president, but his troubles were only beginning.

In the first place there was Zapata.

The First Chief made futile overtures to "the Attila of the South," but Zapata sulked in his mountain hideout and denounced him. "The Plan of Guadalupe is as worthless as Madero's Plan of San Luis Potosi. The only conditions under which I will cooperate with Carranza are complete acceptance of my Plan of Ayala. This and nothing short of this will win my loyalty," Zapata declared.

Because Carranza was incapable of compromise, he gave up all efforts to reconcile with Zapata. He flatly rejected the Plan of Ayala and thus alienated Zapata for good.

Meanwhile, the occupation of Mexico City was marked by wholesale violence, death, and looting. Rebel soldiers and police traded shots due to a misunderstanding. This incident was used as an excuse by Carranza to disband and disarm the police. Once the police were gone, law and order disappeared from Mexico City. Criminals ran wild. Looting was rampant. Nor were common felons the only culprits.

General Obregon took for himself a fine mansion on the fashionable Paseo de la Reforma and confiscated all its belongings for his own use. Several of his officers took over similar residences, while rank-and-file soldiers were content to steal cars, money, jewelry, horses, and anything else of value that came to hand. There also was a good deal of shooting as rebels settled old scores and grudges with long-standing enemies.

"My men are high-spirited. How can I keep them from finishing off their foes?" a rebel officer asked an American journalist.

At its outset, Carranza's regime appeared to be following the pattern of bloodshed that had always scarred Mexico's political scene.

- 27 -

PLOT AND COUNTERPLOT

In the days following Carranza's entry into Mexico City, the political caldron bubbled with trouble. At the city's western fringes, Zapata's ragged men coldly eyed Carranza's troops, and from time to time shots were exchanged as frayed tempers erupted into violence. But the city's outskirts were not the only places where danger stewed and simmered beneath the surface.

Quite unexpectedly, much farther north, full-scale warfare exploded at a town called Naco, which sat astride the United States-Mexican border. Fighting raged between pro-Carranza troops under General Plutarco Calles and forces led by the Villista governor of Sonora state, Jose Maytorena.

Hoping to put out the fire before it became a general conflagration, Obregon asked for and received an audience

171

with Villa in Chihuahua city on August 24. At first all went amicably. The two men traveled together to Naco and worked out a temporary agreement between Calles and Maytorena.

Back in Chihuahua city, Obregon and Villa held additional talks about the need for revolutionary unity. Out of their conferences came a nine-point plan to guide the Revolution into calmer waters. The main stress of their program was that Carranza should remain only as an interim president and in the near future hold free elections in which he would not be a presidential candidate.

Obregon left Chihuahua city and reached the capital on September 9, intending to show Carranza the plan. But the First Chief had already taken steps to stymie Obregon and Villa. Rejecting the plan offhand, he advised Obregon that he was calling an assemblage of Constitutionalist leaders on October 1 to determine the course of the Revolution. "That is not an issue to be decided in secret by a couple of generals," Carranza said righteously.

He was quite certain about any decisions the October 1 meeting might make. The delegates would back him one hundred percent, since they were to be handpicked Carranzistas. Undoubtedly, the First Chief had started on the path to become Mexico's newest dictator.

The tenuous peace up in Sonora ended as fighting between Calles and Maytorena resumed. Once again Obregon hurried to Chihuahua city for further talks with Villa. This time their meetings were not so cordial. Villa launched a tirade at Obregon, accusing him of being a double-crosser. "Calles is your man!" Villa shouted. "He would do nothing without your approval!" With that, Villa called to an aide, "Take this bastard Obregon out and shoot the dirty traitor!" But before the order could be obeyed, Villa calmed down and shook hands with the startled Obregon.

During the next three days, Obregon and Villa reached an accord. At Villa's behest, Obregon had sent

Calles a telegram, ordering him to break off the fighting. Villa was unaware that the wire was in a code known only to Obregon and Calles. What seemed to be asking Calles to obey the cease-fire agreement actually said just the opposite.

Although Obregon lacked the authority to do so, he invited Villa to the October 1 conference. Refusing to go in person, Villa assigned three of his generals instead. Meanwhile, in Mexico City, Carranza had learned of the row between Obregon and Villa. According to his informant, Obregon was under arrest and slated for execution. Fearful that this augured an attack on Mexico City by the Division of the North, Carranza cut all communications with Chihuahua city and tore up twenty miles of railroad track on the main line leading to the national capital.

When Villa heard about this, he once again accused Obregon of "treachery" and arranged to have him quietly liquidated. But there was a leak and Obregon escaped. He was now Villa's sworn enemy.

Enemies were nothing new in Pancho's life. He took on Obregon as he had taken on all the others. Carranza's move to cut off Chihuahua city from the capital ended any indecision Villa might have been harboring about turning against the First Chief. All doubts were cast aside when Villa sent the Division of the North marching toward Mexico City on the morning of September 30. He had given his men a single order: "Crush Carranza!"

As his troops were set in motion, Villa issued a proclamation entitled "Manifesto to the Mexican People" calling upon the masses to help him in the "noble crusade of replacing the dictatorship of the First Chief with a democratic civilian government."

Now that Villa had taken the irrevocable step of seeking to overthrow Carranza, the time had come for his officers and his generals to choose sides. Most of his leaders stayed with him; the mighty Division of the North backed him to the man—but there were some defectors among the officers. Maclovio Herrera refused to march against Carranza, as did several other old-timers who gave as their reason that they were "tired of war."

Moving from Torreon, Villa's troops soon were at the gates of Zacatecas. When they had reached this far south, some of Carranza's backers scrambled about to find a means of reconciling Villa and the First Chief.

When a delegation with this purpose in mind came to him, Villa said, "I want nothing for myself. I want only to rid the country of Carranza. Go tell the First Chief that I will join him in a suicide pact. Tell him that I propose not only that he and I leave the country, but also that we depart this life together!"

Carranza received this suggestion with something less than enthusiasm. However, peace-minded Constitutionalists still sought a way to prevent further bloodshed. One idea was to call a full convention representing all elements of the Revolution, including Villistas and Zapatistas, to be held in Aguascalientes, a town 330 miles northwest of Mexico City. The meeting was to begin October 10, 1914; its purpose: to achieve revolutionary unity and definite plans for the future of Mexico.

Aguascalientes would be preceded by Carranza's Mexico City convention on October 1. Although the later assemblage would reduce the importance of the earlier one, arrangements went on anyway. A less stubborn man than Carranza would simply have called off the October 1 conclave.

It was a lackluster affair, with dull, windy speeches that bored the seventy-nine delegates. The so-called high point of the convention was an appearance by Carranza. He wore a blue suit and a blue peaked cap that made him look like "a steward on a cheap ocean liner," according to a newsman who was present.

The First Chief stood before the delegates and offered to resign. As he had expected, this gesture was unanimously rejected. Then, after thanking the convention for its "vote of confidence," he trudged out of the hall. After accomplishing absolutely nothing, the meeting adjourned on October 5, and all eyes turned to the pleasant town of Aguascalientes, where the fate of the country might well be decided in only five days' time.

- 28 -

THE CONVENTION
OF AGUASCALIENTES

Aguascalientes, a quiet health resort usually frequented by aged and ailing people seeking respite from aches and ills in the curative hot sulfur waters of the spas, assumed a far different aspect on October 10. The tree-lined streets were busy with sturdy men in a motley assortment of military uniforms. Bars, cantinas, restaurants, and promenades overflowed with robust, healthy men—not wan and sickly ones.

In English, Aguascalientes literally means "hot waters." Seldom has a place been more aptly named. Right from the outset, the delegates to the convention were in hot water. The town was host to the most unusual conclave ever held in Mexico's colorful and turbulent history.

The convention was housed in the Morelos Theater, to which delegates flocked, carrying rifles and wearing pistols. Applause for speeches was signified by pounding rifle butts on the floor or firing revolvers into the ceiling.

Martin Luis Guzman, a delegate, later wrote:

I had only to take one look at that assembly to be convinced that little would come of its deliberations. . . . It lacked the civic consciousness and the farseeing patriotism needed at that moment. It was a tragedy in fact, if not in form, with its fatal struggle between two irreconcilable forces. Two profound aspects of the same nationality were locked here in a death struggle.

The start of the convention seemed to belie Guzman's gloomy assessment of it. A Carranzista, Antonio Villareal, was named convention president by acclamation. Then, one by one, the 152 delegates present filed to the stage and autographed the huge Mexican flag standing there. Villistas and Carranzistas exchanged abrazos and everything appeared to be off to a flying start in an aura of goodwill.

Further proceedings were held up because the Zapatista delegation did not show up. Without them, the fabric of unity could not be woven, for Zapata was still in revolt against Carranza.

On October 16, the delegates decided that every effort must be made to persuade Zapata to send the delegation. That day the convention voted that General Felipe Angeles should go to Cuernavaca to convince Zapata that it would be advantageous for him to have representation at Aguascalientes.

The following day Villa rode in from his temporary headquarters in Guadalupe. In an emotional scene at the Morelos Theater, he took an oath of allegiance to the convention amid the crackling of pistol shots and shouts of "Viva Villa!" Pancho then delivered an almost incoherent speech that was made even more unintelligible because he broke down and wept several times. However, his garbled remarks were greeted by thunderous applause. Afterward, outside the theater, he exchanged rib-cracking abrazos with Obregon.

Carranza, on the other hand, refused either to attend the convention or even to send a representative. He had sound political reasons for not doing so. Had he dispatched a spokesman to Aguascalientes, it would have meant that he recognized the legality of the convention— something Carranza did not choose to do.

This behavior by the First Chief alienated the delegates, and every mention of his name brought boos, hisses, catcalls, and curses. By boycotting the convention, Carranza lost more ground and prestige than he possibly could have gained.

Good news came from Angeles in Cuernavaca. He wired that he would be coming back to Aguascalientes with twenty-five Zapatista delegates, including five generals and sixteen colonels. He arrived on October 25 and the Zapatistas entered the Morelos Theater, as one observer recalled, "like soldiers passing through an area of potential ambush."

They were a weirdly garbed group wearing huge sombreros, skintight trousers, and peasant blouses. Even their leader, thirty-year-old Antonio Diaz Soto y Gama, a well-known lawyer, wore the same attire.

The convention came alive with rhetoric and angry words once the Zapatistas were seated. They tried immediately to take over the convention by demanding acceptance of the plan of Ayala. Their shouts of *"Tierra y libertad!"* rattled the theater windows.

As spokesman for the Zapatistas, Diaz Soto y Gama took the floor. He started his speech mildly enough. He said the delegates must listen to their hearts and not be influenced by Carranza, Villa, or anyone else. He told them to take as examples humanity's greatest leaders: Buddha, Christ, Karl Marx, St. Francis of Assisi, and Emiliano Zapata.

Then, suddenly, he grabbed the Mexican flag that bore the signatures of the delegates, crumpled it in his hand, and cried: "What is the good of this dyed rag,

177

bedaubed with the image of a bird of prey? How is it possible, men of the Revolution, that for a hundred years we have been venerating this silly mummery, this lie?" His words brought pandemonium to the floor. Men leaped onto the stage and wrenched the banner from his grip. Others jumped up and down, howling in anger, shouting, cursing, shaking fists, and waving loaded pistols. At any moment bullets seemed likely to fly, and more cautious spectators dived under their seats for cover.

Throughout this uproar, Diaz Soto stood sneering, ignoring the sea of threatening weapons. When the tumult abated, he said, "Now, I shall go on." He sought to soften his speech, his calumny of the flag, but the damage had been done. Any chance the Zapatistas might have had to obtain status in the convention had vanished.

According to a journalist, "Diaz Soto talked too much, heaping abuse and scorn upon his listeners as unfeelingly as though he were unloading garbage. . . . He explained his contempt for the delegates by announcing that he was an anarchist and approved of none but those following his philosophy."

The delegates regarded Diaz Soto and his comrades as erratic extremists. Thus, when the Zapatistas allied with the Villistas, more conservative delegates decided to back Carranza. With a few intemperate words, the opportunity to weld genuine revolutionary unity was lost.

But it was Carranza who struck the match that ignited another civil war. On October 29, he sent a message to the convention, which Obregon read to the meeting. Carranza said that if they regarded him as an obstacle to unity, he was "disposed to retire." However, he set one condition—if he quit, so must Villa and Zapata.

This incensed the Villistas and the Zapatistas because Carranza had lumped their leaders with himself as stumbling blocks to a united front. Delegates, jeering, catcalling, and heckling, rose in support or protest of the First Chief. A dozen fistfights broke out. Knives and revolvers were brandished, but miraculously no blood was shed.

Somehow the chairman restored a semblance of order and the business of the convention proceeded. In a secret ballot, the delegates voted for the retirement of both Villa and Carranza, but took no stand on Zapata. When advised of the convention's decision, Villa declared: "Those cowards didn't go far enough. I propose not only that the convention retire Carranza from his post in exchange for retiring me from mine, but that the convention order both of us to be shot. I will go to any lengths to rid my Mexico of Carranza."

The convention stretched on into November and started procedures to replace Carranza by naming its own provisional president. After much argument and some fisticuffs, the delegates elected a compromise candidate on November 2. He was Eulalio Gutierrez, a man acceptable to everyone but the Zapatistas. Gutierrez had a good record as a minor figure of the Revolution. Formerly a fisherman, stevedore, shopkeeper, and small-time lawyer, he had been a brave fighter for the cause, serving at the front as a dinamitero.

But knowing how to use explosives expertly did not qualify Gutierrez for the complex task that had been imposed upon him. He had little or no political experience. He was honorable and courageous, but that was all. To save Mexico from chaos, the convention had to produce a giant and instead it brought forth a pygmy.

On November 3, Alvaro Obregon was sent to Mexico City to tell Carranza that he had been replaced. However, the First Chief was not in the capital; nor did he remain in one spot long enough for Obregon to catch up with him. This cat-and-mouse game went on for a few days until Carranza, whose people at Aguascalientes had told him about Gutierrez, wrote to the convention. He declared that since the conditions of his retirement had not been met, he was not quitting his office. Besides, he claimed, state governors and military men had pledged to support him.

This letter blew the lid off the convention. On November 5, the executive committee gave Carranza five days to yield. At the same time, Villa, despite all his big talk about suicide and sacrifice for the good of the country, made no move to give up his command. "I'll go when Carranza goes and not a damned second sooner," Pancho snarled.

To show that he could not be pushed out, Villa moved his Division of the North some miles closer to Aguascalientes, which did nothing to allay mounting tensions.

Despite every exhortation from the convention, Carranza remained unmoved. He announced that he would heed no orders from the convention—a body he had never recognized in the first place. When the ultimatum ran out, Gutierrez declared Carranza in rebellion and put Villa in command of the loosely knit Army of the Convention, which was made up of former Constitutionalist divisions.

Once the die had been cast, a number of officers decided to stay with Carranza. When the convention adjourned on November 13, the delegates who still favored the First Chief had fled Aguascalientes and followed him into rebellion. Those who remained backed Villa; civil war once again beclouded Mexican skies. Alvaro Obregon became the most crucial figure in the picture. He had tried to find a peaceful solution and forge unity; but when Gutierrez selected Villa to lead the Army of the Convention, Obregon returned to Carranza's fold. Without Obregon, his talent and troops, Carranza could not have survived. With him, the First Chief had gained the most valuable ally he could recruit.

On November 19, in Mexico City, Obregon declared war on Villa. Simultaneously, he prepared to evacuate the capital, which was being menaced by the powerful Division of the North. Leaving behind only a skeleton garrison under General Luis Blanco, Obregon and the

Carranzista officials trekked to Cordoba, where the First Chief had set up headquarters.

Carranza now headed a government that lacked an important center as its seat. But the Americans gave him one by unexpectedly withdrawing from Veracruz.

- 29 -

"THE ROULETTE WHEELS OF REBELLION"

The Americans in Veracruz had passed the months tediously in the occupied port. The greatest problem they faced was to keep busy. At the end of May, the rainy season had started. Ordinarily, it brought swarms of mosquitoes bearing malaria and yellow fever. But the Americans did something to prevent that peril.

Soldiers and a large force of Mexican laborers were put to work in a massive cleanup campaign. The most stringent sanitary regulations were rigidly observed, especially in public markets, which were "incredibly filthy" according to American standards. Stiff fines and even jail sentences were imposed on all who broke the new rules.

To combat malaria and yellow fever, pools of stagnant water were drained or doused with crude oil to smother disease-bearing mosquito larvae. As a result, malaria, which previously had always reached epidemic proportions, became virtually nonexistent and yellow fever disappeared entirely.

Garbage was regularly collected and the vultures of Veracruz—known for centuries as "nature's garbage men"—found such lean pickings that they migrated to other parts where the scavenging was plentiful.

The Americans repaired battle damage, put in good street lighting, paved roadways, built bridges, modernized the water supply, and laid sewer pipes. Schools reopened, postal service was restored, police and fire units were improved. According to a historian, "The Americans imposed despotism on Veracruz . . . but it was a benevolent despotism . . . in fact, providing the best government the town ever had known."

On September 16, Mexico's Independence Day, the United States government had announced to Carranza that American troops would be withdrawn from Veracruz. But pulling them out proved more difficult and complicated than putting them in. Numbers of Huertistas had taken refuge in the port and the Constitutionalists threatened that severe measures would be taken against them, as well as against those who had collaborated with the gringos during the occupation.

President Wilson tried to get guarantees of safe-conduct for all Mexicans in Veracruz; Carranza refused to give them. Because of this, the American exit was delayed. Then came the added complication of Carranza's replacement by Gutierrez. Wilson now did not know to whom the port should be surrendered.

Eventually, Carranza knuckled under to the American president and promised safety for everyone in Veracruz. Since the convention also had given the same assurances, the White House ordered the evacuation of American forces from Veracruz on November 13. However, Wilson did not give instructions as to which side should get the port.

"Whoever gets here first with the most can have this hellhole," General Funston told a journalist.

Actually, the Carranzistas had troops closer to Veracruz and could move in when the last American left. Early on November 23, the withdrawal began. With troops marching out behind massed bands, the Yankee pullout soon ended. By evening, Carranza, a large body of his troops, the piles of garbage, the fly-ridden markets, and the vultures were back in Veracruz.

Despite his promises, Carranza dealt severely with the refugees and all other Mexicans who had "collaborated" with the gringos. Execution squads worked overtime liquidating those "enemies of the Republic" not able to get out in time.

Even as Carranza was reestablishing himself in Veracruz, Zapata's men were taking over Mexico City. The terrified civilian populace wondered what was in store; frightful tales of Zapatista atrocities stirred understandable fear among the capital's residents.

But the Zapatistas—described by an American resident as "little brown fellows with cartridge belts buckled around gaunt bellies"—shambled into the city, apparently more awed by their strange surroundings than the inhabitants were of the invaders. The simple mountain men stared in wonder at the capital's grand structures and eyed the marvelously stocked shopwindows. The people of Mexico City need not have been afraid. The Zapatistas did not loot stores or homes, but went from door to door humbly asking for a little food because their own meager rations had been exhausted. Some begged in the streets for a peso; they had not been paid in months.

However, when it came to stealing horses, these same meek Zapatistas threw off all restraints. Horses were something familiar, something of practical use. They combed the city searching out horses and took them at will.

Zapata himself arrived in Mexico City on November 26. He stayed only three days, avoided all public appearances, and did not even go near the National Palace. After consulting with some of his commanders, Zapata scurried back to his beloved mountains. "I can't abide the city! To me it is worse than a prison!" he said. But he could not hide forever in the mountains. Villa was nearing Mexico City with his Division of the North and Zapata had to meet him. However, he would not go back into the capital and instead made a rendezvous with Villa at Xochimilco, twelve miles south of Mexico City.

Villa kept the date, arriving with an escort of a dozen Dorados. Zapata greeted him cordially. The two were an odd pair: Villa, tall and swarthy, wearing a battered tropical pith helmet, a loose woolen sweater, khaki cavalry breeches, and riding boots; Zapata, neatly turned out in black coat, blue silk handkerchief, lavender shirt, well-fitting trousers, cowboy boots, and a wide sombrero.

After exchanging the traditional abrazos, the two revolutionaries talked. They finally agreed to make a joint entry into Mexico City on Sunday, December 6, 1914. Zapata called for a bottle of brandy and, though Villa ordinarily did not drink, he joined in a toast to the Revolution.

The December 6 occupation of the capital was a grand affair. The parade started early in the morning and wound up at dusk. The city's residents welcomed Villa and Zapata with cheers and flowers; it was a day of triumph for the Revolution and the two leaders.

That evening Eulalio Gutierrez, the provisional president, gave a banquet in the National Palace. Casting aside his customary shyness, Zapata attended the affair, sharing the head of the table with Villa. Everyone present had a good time: generals, politicians, foreign diplomats, and civilian guests.

The next day, Villa and Zapata called on Gutierrez. By then, the festive glow of the previous night had worn off. The two leaders had come to tell Gutierrez how they were going to campaign against Carranza and brushed off all his suggestions. By their actions Villa and Zapata demonstrated that they regarded Gutierrez as a figure-head and a person of no importance.

The plan concocted by the two rebel chieftains was that Villa should drive southeast toward Veracruz while Zapata pushed in the same direction by way of Puebla. After their meeting with Gutierrez, Villa and Zapata parted with a show of warm comradeship.

They were never to meet again.

As 1914 entered its final weeks, the situation in Mexico was one of complete confusion. Generals, colonels, and commanders of armed groups waited indecisively, not sure which side to join. All northern Mexico was a crazy quilt of factions aligned either with Villa and Zapata or with Carranza. A historian of the period wrote: "The supreme gamble of the Mexican officer was whether to join the revolt against the government or participate in its suppression. In the roulette wheels of rebellion, the officer staked dishonorable death against a promotion ... the men who reached divisional generalship were those who placed their swords on the winning number."

Had Villa and Zapata, whose combined armies numbered more than sixty thousand fighting men, carried out the plan for a combined thrust at Veracruz, Carranza would have been overthrown with ease. But, after taking Puebla in late December, Zapata brought his advance to a halt some two hundred miles short of Veracruz.

Zapata stopped because neither he nor his soldiers cared to go beyond the borders of Morelos state. That was their turf; anything beyond it was unknown and somewhat frightening to them. They actually were not interested in what happened to the rest of Mexico. Morelos was Mexico and Mexico was Morelos as far as the Zapatistas were concerned. Once Morelos was freed, the Revolution was over for them. Thus, after taking Puebla, Zapata made no further move and was a useless ally to Villa.

Villa also made a tactical blunder. Instead of driving right on to Veracruz, he had second thoughts over taking such a daring stroke. He fumbled about making certain his supply lines to Chihuahua city and Torreon were secure. For once, Villa showed surprising timidity, unlike his usually rash style. Those who knew him were puzzled by his reluctance to advance on Veracruz. But the flamboyant leader's hesitancy was easily explained. He knew little or nothing about southern Mexico; the rugged north was his country. To him, Veracruz was alien territory. He was a simple man, like Zapata, and cared more about his home ground than Mexico as a whole.

So, instead of mopping up the Carranzistas, Villa wasted the month of December 1914 in Mexico City. His time was spent in high living, and many convention officers followed his example.

In shocking contrast to their orderly and bloodless entry into the capital, the Villistas and Zapatistas unleashed a reign of terror remarkable for its ferocity. Mass arrests and mass murders became commonplace. A flood of debauchery and crime engulfed the city. As one observer said, "The three R's in Mexico City were Robbery, Rape, and Revenge. No matter what a Villista or Zapatista did, he went unpunished. Restraints were cast aside. Crime and criminality became the way of life."

Recalling December 1914, a participant wrote: "Those were the days when murders and robberies were like the striking of a clock, marking the hours that passed."

By the end of December, Provisional President Gutierrez could take no more. He decided to form a new coalition that would eliminate Carranza, Villa, and Zapata. Toward this end, he got in touch with Obregon and other generals he believed might go along with him. Senor Gutierrez was playing a dangerous game.

"I WANT TO FREE MY CONSCIENCE"

At the time Gutierrez was making contact with Obregon, Pancho Villa was out of Mexico City, visiting Guadalajara. Unhappily for Gutierrez, Villa's spies were everywhere, and word of the provisional president's activities soon reached Pancho.

His reactions were predictable. First he flew into a monumental rage. Then he calmed down and ordered all exits from Mexico City sealed off so that Gutierrez could not escape. Next, Villa hurried back to the capital and called a meeting of the Convention's executive committee, at which he scathingly denounced Gutierrez, accusing him of planning to desert to Carranza. Villa's speech was so violent that several members of the committee, fearful they would be shot along with Gutierrez, went into hiding.

After the meeting, Villa stormed up to Gutierrez's house, accompanied by his triggerman, Fierro, and a squad of Dorados. Drawing his revolver, Villa pounded on the door with the gun butt. Gutierrez answered. He might have been politically naïve, but did not lack nerve. As Villa shouted, ranted, threatened, and cursed, Gutierrez eyed him unflinchingly and denied he was going over to Carranza. He did admit that he had intended to leave Mexico City, but only because no one obeyed him as president of the Convention government.

"I want to free my conscience of the crimes you are committing in the name of the government I am supposed to head," Gutierrez snapped. "And if you want to make something of that—then do so!"

Gutierrez's resoluteness impressed Villa, who calmed down. This confrontation, much to Fierro's disappointment, ended in crunching abrazos. However, Gutierrez realized he had been spared only because of Villa's quixotic needs.

Ignoring the peril he already faced, Gutierrez continued to communicate with Obregon, seeking to persuade him and other "sensible revolutionaries" to form a new coalition. This was learned when General Angeles captured some documents after a battle with Generals Villareal and Maclovio Herrera, both former Villistas. The papers seized included some letters from Gutierrez to Villareal proposing ways to get rid of Villa and Carranza.

Angeles showed the letters to Villa, who immediately telegraphed Jose Robles, an old comrade, in Mexico City, ordering the instant execution of Gutierrez. However, Robles had had enough of blood; besides, he liked Gutierrez. Instead of carrying out his order, Robles warned Gutierrez and cast in his lot with the provisional president.

The only logical move for both men was to get out of Mexico City. Before daybreak, January 10, 1915, Gutierrez, Robles, several other politicians, and three brigades commanded by General Luis Blanco escaped from the capital in a northeasterly direction. Blanco had switched from Obregon to Villa and now changed sides again. In his escape, Gutierrez showed himself to be a lot shrewder than anyone had thought. He took with him thirteen million pesos from the treasury, leaving less than half that amount behind.

His journey was a difficult one. The escort gradually fell away until only a handful of followers was left. At last they reached a desert hamlet called Doctor Arroyo, a place so isolated and insignificant that not even Villa bothered him there. In that godforsaken spot Gutierrez stayed on, unnoticed, still dreaming of one day uniting

Mexico. Eventually, he disappeared into obscurity along with the thirteen million pesos.

The Convention of Aguascalientes reconvened on January 16 to name a new provisional president. The man it chose was a twenty-nine-year-old Villista, Roque Gonzalez Garza, who formed a government larded with Villa's backers. Acting with great energy, Gonzalez Garza declared martial law in Mexico City and its environs. He also tried to do something about the depleted treasury. But the currency mess grew worse. During the next few months, first one faction, then another, held Mexico City. Paper money became worthless as each side repudiated the money issued by the other. Soon merchants were refusing to accept paper and would take only gold or silver.

Meanwhile, further complications had developed. Fighting had again broken out in Naco on the United States border. Shooting was furious in the Mexican section of the town. However, bullets recognized no boundary lines. Although Naco's American district was plainly marked with a row of flags, damage was caused there by shot and shell. Wooden houses were riddled. Every window facing Mexico was blocked with bales of hay, mattresses, steel plates, or planking.

American casualties were mounting as the Naco fight roared on. Several townspeople had been wounded. The U.S. Tenth Cavalry camp near the town had been hit so often that the regimental commander moved the bivouac a mile northward. By January 1915, the situation had become intolerable, and General Hugh Scott, now the Army chief of staff, came from Washington to see if he could negotiate some sort of settlement.

Hard pressed by Maytorena, Plutarco Calles agreed at once to give up Naco; all he asked was safe-conduct for his men and himself. On the other hand, Maytorena, already tasting victory, refused to cooperate. He told Scott that the fighting had cost him eight hundred men and he refused to make that sacrifice with nothing to show for it.

General Scott then called for a meeting with Villa. Once again, the two men met at midpoint on the international bridge between Ciudad Juarez and El Paso. Scott firmly warned that unless fighting ceased immediately, he was going to take drastic measures. Without actually mentioning it, the general implied intervention by United States troops. Villa argued for time, claiming he could clean out the Carranzistas in eight hours.

"I don't give a damn if you can do it in eight minutes," Scott bellowed. "I won't allow another shot to be fired in Naco! Damn it, American lives are at stake!"

After that outburst, Villa gave in and promised that Maytorena's forces would fall back from the border. The agreement papers were brought to Maytorena for signature on January 9, 1915. He scribbled his name, flung the pen to the floor, and burst into tears of rage and frustration. But the next day, in accordance with the terms, Calles withdrew to Agua Prieta, while Maytorena moved westward to Nogales. For the moment, at least, peace reigned on the United States-Mexican border.

- 31 -

"THEY FLEE AT THE JINGLE
OF MY SPURS"

While Villa was occupied in the north, Obregon and Carranza were making good use of the breathing spell they had been granted. For once in his life, Carranza was amenable to advice. He accepted Obregon's recommendations for a program of sweeping social reforms in order to attract backers among the peons and workers.

Among the reforms Carranza pledged were land distribution, better living conditions, a revised electoral system, the abolition of peonage, and minimum standards of wages and hours. He also promised freedom for trade union organization. This won him the support of Mexico's largest trade union, Casa del Obrero Mundial, which recruited six battalions of young workers to fight for Carranza.

Obregon was given command of the Constitutionalist army, renamed the Army of Operations. He injected fresh vigor into the troops and on January 5 led them to victory by taking Puebla from the Zapatistas in a daylong battle. Not pausing to rest, Obregon pushed a second column to within sixty miles of Mexico City. A few days later, he was only thirty miles from the capital and still advancing.

This so disconcerted the Zapatistas in the city's garrison that they pulled out and retired to their mountain strongholds in Morelos. Convention officials followed them and reconvened in Cuernavaca. They left Mexico City just in time, for, on January 28, Obregon's ten-thousand-man Army of Operations entered the city.

It was apparent from the start that Obregon intended to hold the capital only temporarily. He made no attempt to drive away Zapatista elements hovering at the outskirts; nor did Carranza return to the national capital. The First Chief preferred the security of Veracruz, and even announced that the port would be the new capital of Mexico.

He hoped this might bring the foreign diplomatic corps from Mexico City to Veracruz, thus gaining implied recognition of his regime. But foreigners preferred the cosmopolitan pleasures of Mexico City to Veracruz with its bad climate and small-town diversions. Within a few weeks, Carranza and everyone else had forgotten the whole idea and Mexico City remained the capital of the strife-torn country.

Once in Mexico City, Obregon behaved like a conqueror, not a liberator. He stripped the capital of everything worth taking. Factory machinery was dismantled and shipped off to Veracruz. Cars and horses were confiscated. Schools were closed and the teachers forcibly removed to Veracruz. An American resident has recalled, "It was unsafe to go outside. Obregon's scavengers were liable to take the clothes off your back."

Obregon decreed Villista currency worthless and made Carranzista currency the only legal tender. This brought hardship to the capital's businessmen, banks, and merchants. The city teetered on the brink of economic disaster. When banks and businesses closed in protest, they were forced to reopen at gunpoint.

Shortages of food and water became serious. The Zapatistas had blown up the main water-pumping station in Xochimilco and pressure in the pipes was reduced to such a trickle that water flowed from taps only between 5:00 and 6:00 A.M. daily. Because the pressure was so low, sewage could not be flushed and the city was "oppressed by an assortment of foul stenches which made one gag with every breath," a diplomat reported.

With the Zapatistas blocking off the city's western approaches, food could be brought only from the east, and in limited quantities. Speculators, hoarders, and black marketeers gained control of dwindling foodstuffs and sold them at inflated prices payable in gold or silver.

By the end of February, only the rich could afford to eat regularly.

According to an American resident, "Stray cats and dogs vanished from the streets. Certain stalls in the nearly deserted public markets sold what they called 'special meat' . . . Everyone knew they had butchered the dogs and cats of Mexico City's alleys. The city was filthy . . . and in one district, an epidemic of typhus raged. . . . Poor people starved to death. In all her history Mexico City never had suffered such hardships."

The Roman Catholic church was one institution that felt Obregon's harsh hand. For more than a hundred years the church had backed the wrong side in Mexico's political struggles. Father Hidalgo and Father Morelos, who had led the revolt against Spain in 1810, had been excommunicated. The church had supported Maximilian and the French against Benito Juarez, just as it had the Diaz and Huerta dictatorships. Now, with an anticlerical like Obregon in control of Mexico City, the church reaped the harvest of its past misjudgment.

Since childhood, Obregon had opposed the church. He was not against Catholicism, but the involvement of the church in politics. As a revolutionary, he counted the church among the foes of the Revolution. In a newspaper interview on February 21, 1915, Obregon called the church a "malignant tumor" and, while conceding that there were some well-intentioned clergymen, stated that they were so few that the "wickedness of the rest erases the good the minority might do."

Given a free hand by their commander, Obregon's soldiers rampaged through the city's churches, looting and vandalizing. The fashionable Santa Brigida Cathedral was ransacked. Statues were smashed, holy objects broken, stained-glass windows shattered.

Besides destroying and damaging church property, Obregon demanded 2.5 million pesos from the Archdiocese of Mexico City "to alleviate the distress of the working classes." He gave the church officials five days to raise the money and when it had not been produced at the deadline date, February 19, Obregon summoned all leading clergymen to the National Palace. But only 168 of the 400 priests in the city turned up. These he arrested and held as hostages until the money was paid. However, the church hierarchy held firm and refused to hand over a single peso.

Businessmen also were given bad treatment. Obregon imposed crushing taxes on them. When they held a protest meeting at the Hidalgo Theater, Obregon came to address the gathering. "Don't worry about this newest tax. It's nothing compared to what I have in store for you!" he told the audience.

Obregon's attitude toward church and business aroused strong feelings against him in the United States, Great Britain, and other countries with commercial interests in Mexico. President Wilson, through Secretary of State Bryan, warned that under the circumstances the United States would not stand "idly by."

The bogeyman of American intervention had appeared again.

But by March 9, Obregon's grip on Mexico City loosened. All prisoners—businessmen and clergy—were released, and the next evening the Army of Operations left the capital by train for Pachuca, in the northeast. Villa was advancing in that direction and Obregon was moving to block him.

As the Army of Operations left, wary Zapatista advance guards entered the city. Universal relief swept the populace. Church bells rang for the first time in weeks, clanging a joyous welcome to the Zapatistas.

But actual possession of Mexico City had little strategic value at the time. Obregon had stayed only long enough to plunder the capital. Villa saw no purpose in holding it. The Zapatistas were the only faction eager to have Mexico City. The Convention, now meeting in Cuernavaca, had become dominated by Zapata's people. It voted to return to Mexico City and, on March 21, the Convention government was back with its new provisional president, Roque Gonzalez Garza.

The Zapatistas restored services in Mexico City.

Water flowed normally again, foodstuffs poured into the capital, and the Villista *dos caras* currency was legal tender once more.

On this return to Mexico City, the Zapatistas took up where they had left off and violated private property. The swanky country club was converted to a barracks, its opulent ballroom a stable. Residences were seized for military use. The ground floors of elegant mansions housed horses, while upper floors served as billets for Zapatistas and their women. The churches Obregon had failed to loot were sacked and many were set afire.

Emiliano Zapata took no part in these doings, nor did he even come to Mexico City. He sat in his mountain retreat, not even lifting a finger to help ease the worsening military situation around the capital. The winds were shifting against Convention fortunes.

Obregon maneuvered the Army of Operations from Pachuca to Celaya, which put him on Villa's flank. At the end of March, the Convention delegates registering in Mexico City suddenly realized they had been cut off from Villa. For several days they argued about what was to be done. Some favored moving to Villa-controlled territory and setting up at Chihuahua city. But by then it was too late; Obregon had cut off the northerly escape routes. All communications between Mexico City and Villa were broken.

For the first time since the start of the Revolution in 1910, Pancho Villa found himself in bad military shape. On January 17–18, 1915, his top commander, Rodolfo Fierro, had lost Guadalajara. Villa was furious over this defeat. He gathered every available man for the recapture of Guadalajara. When he met Fierro, Villa gave his crestfallen favorite a severe tongue-lashing and even threatened to have him shot. But after a time he forgave Fierro, warning him to do better next time.

Villa retook Guadalajara on February 12, but before his men could recover from that battle, a hurried call for help came from General Felipe Angeles on the defensive in Monterrey. He was being menaced by three Carranzista armies under Pablo Gonzalez, Maclovio Herrera, and Antonio Villareal.

Villa responded at once to Angeles. He regrouped his troops and made Fierro stop shooting all the prisoners taken at Guadalajara. The bloodthirsty Fierro wanted revenge against those who had defeated him.

"Don't be a fool, Rodolfo," Villa said. "Every man you kill now is one less to work for us repairing the railroad. Wait until the tracks are fixed—then shoot them."

Villa left Fierro to defend Guadalajara and moved out to join Angeles at Monterrey. Arriving there, he urged Angeles to attack and quickly routed the besiegers. Pleased at the easy victory, Villa strutted about crowing to Angeles, "You see, Senor General! They flee at the jingle of my spurs!"

However, his jubilation swiftly evaporated at the news that Fierro again had been defeated, with the loss of two thousand men, eight hundred horses, and the city of Guadalajara.

- 32 -

THE CRUCIAL BATTLES
OF CELAYA

Stung by the latest setback at Guadalajara, Villa wanted a spectacular victory. Rallying his weary men, he plunged southward and came upon Obregon dug in at Celaya, a town some 150 miles northwest of Mexico City.

The terrain around Celaya was ideal for defense; the uneven ground was laced with canals and irrigation ditches. Obregon utilized every defensive possibility. He was advised by a German officer, Colonel Maximilian Kloss, fresh from the battlefields of France.

Kloss showed Obregon how to dig trenches and machine gun emplacements protected by successive aprons of barbed wire. Colonel Kloss utilized all the experience he had gathered after a year of trench warfare in France.

Villa neither knew nor cared about these tactics, and went on to attack Obregon in his old way. His men easily overran Obregon's lightly held outposts. On April 6, 1915, Villa ordered a golpe terrifico aimed at smashing through the main defenses of Celaya. The Division of the North gave the best it had to give. But cavalry horses and infantrymen became ensnarled in the barbed wire, offering perfect targets for enfilading machine guns, which mowed them down in windrows. Villa lost the cream of the Division of the North—his Dorados, who were almost wiped out in the futile onslaught. The attackers stumbled away, leaving more than a thousand of their comrades dead on the wire.

But Villa's men still had fight in them. At daybreak, April 7, another mass assault swept down on Celaya like a human tidal wave.

In one sector, the wire was breached and machine gun emplacements knocked out. Through this gap, a Villista spearhead poured and burst into the center of Celaya. The Villistas remained only briefly; an Obregon counterattack drove them out with heavy losses.

By noon, the Division of the North had fought itself out. Obregon then delivered his knockout punch. He sent six thousand cavalrymen under General Cesareo Castro into a smashing assault on the Villistas' flank.

Villa had no cavalry to meet this thrust; his own splendid horsemen had been wasted the previous day. Castro's cavalry slashed through Villa's infantry, and

Pancho's only chance was to order a retreat. He managed to extricate all his artillery, but left a field strewn with dead and wounded. Falling back to Irapuato, thirty-eight miles to the west, Villa licked his wounds and prepared for another try at Celaya.

Instead of pursuing the beaten Villistas, Obregon heeded Colonel Kloss and remained at Celaya. He put his men to work improving defensive positions, stringing barbed wire, and digging new trenches. Obregon was confident that Villa would mount another attack; he knew his impetuous foe.

Villa mobilized every gun, shell, bullet, and man at Irapuato, but did not have the patience to await the arrival of General Angeles and the Monterrey garrison. In the past, speed, audacity, and courage had carried Villa on to an unbroken string of victories. But now these same qualities were leading him to certain defeat.

On April 13, only a week after the first battle of Celaya, Villa returned for a second round. His forces numbered more than twenty-five thousand, while Obregon could muster only fifteen thousand. Villa had superiority in artillery and manpower, but Obregon had machine guns, trenches, and Colonel Kloss.

For two days, after vigorous artillery barrages, Villa threw his men against Celaya in massive assaults. But the shells had not breached the wire or even caused many casualties among Obregon's men in their deep trenches and dugouts. Again and again the Villistas reached the wire only to be slaughtered.

But the strain was starting to tell on Obregon's troops. Celaya was aflame from the shelling. Ammunition was running low. A number of machine guns had been knocked out of action.

By April 15, the situation seemed so bad that some of Obregon's officers petitioned him to withdraw. However, Obregon stood fast. He still had his ace in the hole. Castro's cavalry had not yet been committed to the battle.

Once again, as during the previous week, Obregon waited until what he thought was the right moment. Just as the Division of the North came charging out into the open, Obregon sent in his cavalry. The troopers drove the Villistas into panicky flight. Villa's men were routed and the Division of the North collapsed like a pricked balloon.

Villa pulled back in headlong retreat, a withdrawal so precipitous that he had to leave behind twenty-eight of his thirty-four fieldpieces. The second battle of Celaya was a total disaster for him. A neutral observer estimated that the clash had cost him more than four thousand dead and wounded and at least an equal number captured.

Villa and the survivors of his once mighty division struggled northward. He was never to recover from the Celaya debacle. Obregon announced his victory to Carranza and added sardonically, "Fortunately for us, Villa commanded the enemy."

- 33 -

"THERE IS NO END BUT DEATH"

Villa's retreat ended at Aguascalientes. Withdrawing his troops from the western and northeastern fronts, he relieved the pressure on the foe at Tampico and Guadalajara. Obregon's victory also meant that the Carranzistas could retake Mexico City at will. The Convention delegates there, protected only by the Zapatistas, could not remain in the capital much longer. By May, the Convention was hardly functioning.

Villa, fuming in Aguascalientes, vowed to even the

score with Obregon. He grew suspicious of those around him, accusing first this man, then that one, of plotting to betray him. One of his generals, Dionisio Triana, a loyal officer, was unlucky enough to have a cousin serving on Obregon's staff. When this was called to Villa's attention, he sent for the man. Later, Villa wrote: "I saw at a glance that he was a traitor and had him shot as an example for the rest."

Obregon, who now outnumbered Villa, commenced a slow, relentless advance toward Aguascalientes, moving steadily along until he reached Leon, halfway between Celaya and Aguascalientes.

Apparently Villa had not learned anything at Celaya, for he prepared to attack Obregon at Leon. General Angeles tried to dissuade Villa from making such a rash move. "Force Obregon to attack you," Angeles argued. "He'll be at the end of a long supply line which can be cut. We'll have him by the throat."

Villa brushed him off. "I'm a man who came into the world to attack. If I'm defeated by attacking today, I'll win by attacking tomorrow," Villa told Angeles.

On June 3, he foolishly hurled the remnant of his division at Obregon, who was properly entrenched near Leon. The battle for the town was a furious one and almost caused Obregon's death. He was at the front with a group of officers when a shell exploded close by. It tore off his right arm at the elbow. Bleeding profusely and convinced that he was dying, Obregon drew his pistol, put the muzzle to his head, and pulled the trigger. The hammer clicked harmlessly. An orderly had cleaned the weapon that morning and had failed to reload it.

An aide wrenched the pistol from Obregon. The general was rushed to a hospital where surgeons saved his life. Obregon's junior officers took over the Army of Operations and bloodily repulsed Villa.

Recovering rapidly from his wound, Obregon soon was back at the head of his troops, maintaining steady pressure on Villa. Every day Villa's strength dwindled as his broken men, sick of war and defeat, slipped away into the desert.

Among those who decamped after Villa's third defeat was General Tomas Urbina, a longtime comrade. Not only did Urbina desert, but he also took with him Villa's war chest, which contained thousands of pesos in gold. Fleeing to a Durango hideout, Urbina was tracked down by Villa, Fierro, and a handful of surviving Dorados.

They found Urbina at dawn one morning and Fierro wounded him with a single shot. For a moment, Villa was touched by compassion as he looked down at his bleeding friend. He decided against killing Urbina and promised that a doctor would be brought from the closest town.

But that moment of compassion evaporated when only a small portion of the missing gold was found. (Despite assiduous searches throughout the years, the rest of the treasure has never been located. Historians believe that Urbina buried it somewhere in the desert.) Bellowing in rage, Villa turned the wounded Urbina over to Fierro and shouted, "Damn you, Tomas! There is no end but death for a traitor!" With that, he rode off and left Fierro to his favorite pastime—murder.

Because of Obregon's successes in the field, the Carranzista forces virtually cordoned off Mexico City. Once again the food situation grew critical there. But this time, not even the wealthy could buy food—there simply was none to be had. People were known to barter an automobile for a few pounds of meat.

The conditions in Mexico City, real and exaggerated, forced President Wilson to make another policy statement. On June 2, 1915, he declared that the United States "must lend its active moral support to some man or group of men who can rally the suffering Mexican people. . . . I call upon the warring factions in that unfortunate country to resolve their differences quickly. If they cannot do so, within a very short time this government will be constrained to decide what means should be employed by the United States in order to help Mexico save herself and serve her people."

Since Carranza was winning the war, he merely thanked President Wilson for his interest. The Zapatistas ignored his pleas altogether. On the other hand, Villa, who was definitely being beaten, eagerly sought some kind of settlement. He urged all factions to discuss means of bringing peace and justice to Mexico.

Carranza haughtily rebuffed Villa. He knew the way things were: Villa's officers and men were deserting him. It daily was becoming clearer that Carranza was the man the United States would have to recognize.

Confusion spread in Mexico City. On June 9, 1915, the Convention deposed Gonzalez Garza and appointed in his stead an obscure politician named Lagos Chazaro. The reason for the change was that Gonzalez Garza and the Zapatistas had fallen out. The Convention knew Chazaro would give them no trouble.

Three days later word came that Carranza's troops were closing in on Mexico City. Carranza wanted to be there when the Americans recognized him—as he was certain they would.

There followed a bewildering period when first one side, then the other, briefly held the capital. But on August 2 the Convention government finally fled to Morelos, where Zapata still held sway. That same day, Pablo Gonzalez reentered Mexico City at the head of troops known as the Army Corps of the East.

Once again Mexico City had lived through a desperate ordeal.

- 34 -

THE YEARS OF
THE WHIRLWIND

In the summer of 1915, a figure from the past had reentered the scene—none other than General Victoriano Huerta. While in his Barcelona exile, Huerta had been approached by Captain Franz von Rintelen, a German naval officer. Rintelen had an intriguing proposition. Germany would help restore Huerta to power if he promised to promulgate an anti-American policy to divert United States attention from the European war.

Huerta agreed, and there followed a cloak-and-dagger game that seemed lifted from a bad spy novel. Money was passed, secret meetings held, guns and muniitons cached. Huerta was smuggled back to the U.S.-Mexican border where he was to be met by Pascual Orozco, once the leader of the dreaded Colorados.

But all the plotting came to nothing. While trying to sneak into Mexico, Orozco was shot dead in a running gun battle with Texas Rangers. American authorities arrested Huerta and confined him to the stockade in Fort Bliss, Texas, where he contracted yellow jaundice and died on January 14, 1916.

In the meantime, the United States had recognized Carranza, so angering Villa that he turned outlaw again, raided across the United States border, and shot up the town of Columbus, New Mexico. The raid tipped the balance in Washington. General John J. "Black Jack" Pershing, commanding a large force of cavalry, infantry, and artillery, crossed over into Mexico and chased Villa through the northern wastelands.

But the American pursuit was of no avail and the so-called Punitive Expedition was recalled on February 7, 1917. A few months later, Pershing would be commanding the American Expeditionary Force in Europe and the men who had gone after Villa would be fighting and dying in World War I.

On March 11, 1917, elections were held in Mexico and Venustiano Carranza emerged victorious. Now legal president of the Republic, he felt free to show his deep anti-American sentiments by turning to Germany for friendship and help. The Germans wooed him assiduously. They gave him military assistance: Carranza's army soon had more than fifty German advisers; they also gave him financial and technical aid. Indeed, so far had Carranza's pro-Germanism gone that Germany's Foreign Secretary Arthur Zimmermann thought that he might be persuaded to make war on the United States. Zimmermann had sent an encoded telegram to his ambassador in Mexico City suggesting that Carranza should be approached on this matter. He authorized the ambassador to state that Germany would help Mexico regain the territories she had lost to the Americans in the United States-Mexican War of 1845–48.

Zimmermann did not know that the British had broken the German Foreign Office code. The British secret service decoded the telegram and passed the information on to the Americans. The international uproar that arose helped put the United States into the war on the side of the Allies.

Once inaugurated as president, Carranza announced that the Revolution was over. He was wrong. His government was riddled with corruption and discontent rose again. However, Carranza did try to help his country and gave Mexico a liberal constitution that provided benefits for the people never before granted.

Peace was fitful under Carranza. There were minor uprisings and rebellions. Zapata and Villa, both now turned to virtual outlawry, continued to make trouble. Bloody civil war embroiled Morelos, and Carranza organized a full-scale campaign to crush the Zapatistas. That revolt finally ended with the assassination of Zapata. On April 10, 1919, he was tricked into meeting one of Carranza's generals who claimed he wanted to switch to the Zapatista side. The rendezvous was a trap. As Zapata approached, the purportedly defecting troops, drawn up by their commander in parade formation, came to present arms. Suddenly, the front rank leveled their rifles and fired at Zapata, instantly killing him and his escort. With Zapata's death, the revolt in Morelos ended. Now Carranza had only to cope with Villa.

The wily Pancho carried off his raids and banditry with skill and abandon. He led the Carranza troops a merry chase and they never caught up with him. However, from time to time, small groups of his followers were captured and he lost all his refuges in northern Mexico.

In November 1919, General Felipe Angeles, Villa's faithful follower and friend, was captured and sentenced to be shot. The execution was carried out on November 26, in the former Villista stronghold of Chihuahua city. Angeles met death gamely. Not only did he refuse a blindfold, but he also gave the execution squad the order to fire.

Carranza's term of office ended in 1919. A presidential election had been set for June 1920. Alvaro Obregon was among the several candidates. However, before the election date, a revolt against Carranza flared up in Sonora state. It was led by the state governor, Adolfo de la Huerta, who claimed he was "sick and tired" of the corruption in Mexico City. The uprising was soon joined by Obregon. It ended on May 20, 1920, when Carranza, attempting to flee from Mexico City to Veracruz, was caught and shot to death.

The Chamber of Deputies chose Adolfo de la Huerta to serve as interim president until a new one was elected and inaugurated. De la Huerta proved to be a spectacular leader. In a remarkably short time he brought peace to Mexico and even negotiated a surrender deal with Villa. By its terms, Villa was given immunity from prosecution and could retire on a 25,000-acre hacienda that the government provided in an isolated region near Parral. Villa accepted the terms and rode off into retirement.

But Villa's stormy career did not have a tranquil end. In 1923, he was assassinated by an old foe, Jesus Salas Barraza, who lived until 1951 and cried out on his deathbed, "I die serenely for I rid humanity of a monster!"

The election scheduled for June 1920 was finally held on September 5, and resulted in a stunning victory for Alvaro Obregon. After a decade of civil strife, it seemed that Mexico was on the road to a period of peaceful reconstruction. But in Mexico, the throbbing pulse of violence still beat. The Revolution still beckoned men with visions of glory.

Adolfo de la Huerta led a brief uprising in 1924, only to have it put down in crushing style. That same year, Plutarco Calles succeeded Obregon, who was elected again in 1928. (Under the 1917 constitution, the presidential term had been reduced from six to four years.)

However, Obregon was never inaugurated for his second term. A group of religious fanatics, led by a woman known only as Madre Conchita, had vowed to kill him because he had restricted the church. On July 16, 1928, Madre Conchita persuaded a man named Jose de

Leon Toral that killing Obregon would solve all Mexico's problems. He assassinated the president-elect during a political banquet held at a restaurant significantly named La Bombita—the little bomb.

As one historian wrote: "With the death of Obregon, Mexico passed through the years of the whirlwind . . . now [a] calmer breeze blew across the mountains and deserts and lakes and rivers. . . . Violence had bred the Revolution and Revolution had bred violence."

Selected Bibliography

In preparing *Land and Liberty*, the author consulted numerous books, periodicals, newspapers, histories, and journals. Listed below are some books that will give a reader deeper insight into the time of the Mexican Revolution and the personalities involved.

Alba, Victor. *The Mexicans*. London: Pall Mall Press, 1967.

Braddy, Haldeen. *Pershing's Mission in Mexico*. El Paso: Texas Western College Press, 1966.

Bush, Ira Jefferson. *Gringo Doctor*. Caldwell, Ohio: The Caxton Printers Ltd., 1939.

Cline, Howard F. *The U.S. and Mexico*. Cambridge, Mass.: Harvard University Press, 1963.

Guzman, Martin Luis. *The Eagle and the Serpent*. New York: Doubleday, 1965.

Johnson, William Weber. *Heroic Mexico*. New York: Doubleday, 1968.

O'Connor, Richard. *Ambrose Bierce*. London: Gollancz, 1968.

———. *Black Jack Pershing*. New York: Doubleday, 1961.

Strode, Hudson. *Timeless Mexico*. New York: Harcourt, Brace & Co., 1944.

Swarthout, Glendon. *They Came to Cordura*. London: Heinemann, 1958.

Tuchman, Barbara. *The Zimmermann Telegram*. New York: Macmillan, 1958.

Womack, John, Jr. *Zapata and the Mexican Revolution*. New York: Knopf, 1969.

Index

Author's Note

Land and Liberty recounts the story of the Mexican Revolution that started in 1910 and lasted for a turbulent decade marked by bloodshed previously unknown on the American continent. For violence and fury, it exceeded even the Civil War in the United States.

I do not claim that this book is a definitive history of the complex events of the Mexican Revolution. I merely have sought to illuminate that era for young readers. I have neither fictionalized nor dramatized what happened during those years of turmoil. The incidents were dramatic enough, and fiction cannot match truth.

To simplify matters, I have anglicized the spelling of all names and places.

Of course, in preparing a book, every author has help along the lonely road he must travel. I wish to thank those who helped me. I am especially grateful to my agent, Miss Candida Donadio. The good librarians of the New York Historical Society and the New York Public Library deserve a bow for making available much material and giving expert advice.

I would be remiss if I did not thank my editor, Mr. Ron Buehl, who believed—or pretended to believe—my lame excuses for missing deadlines. I also wish to express gratitude to those friends who have stood by me during a time of trial when I sorely needed friends.

Irving Werstein
New York City, 1971